Teaching Harry

Using the Harry Potter series to engage, enrich and extend high ability learners

Selena Gallagher, PhD

This book has not been prepared, authorised, or endorsed by J.K. Rowling, the publishers or distributors of the Harry Potter books, or Warner Bros. Entertainment.

Contents

Introduction

Teaching Harry is an opportunity to work some magic of your own, weaving together J.K. Rowling's spellbinding Harry Potter series with numerous challenging and imaginative activities to inspire and extend your high ability students. Imagine the impact we can have as teachers by introducing our students to this life-changing book series, and by allowing those who have already discovered it for themselves to explore all the depth and complexity it has to offer.

This resource is designed to help you do just that. There are activities here for everyone, whether you are looking for extension activities for an individual student in your class, activities to suit a group of students working together in the regular classroom or in a withdrawal group, students in a camp or other extra-curricular environment, or for a whole-class themed unit. It is anticipated that most of these activities will suit more able students in grades 5 to 9, although this obviously depends on the level of ability of your own group of students. Many activities may also be suitable for older and younger students, but some modification or additional scaffolding may be needed in some instances.

Specific suggestions about how to put the activities in this resource to use in your classroom are set out after we look in more detail at why this incredible series has so much potential to assist your highly able students in their learning.

Why Harry?

Harry Potter is more than a fictional character. He is a cultural phenomenon. J.K. Rowling's seven-book series has sold more than 400 million copies, been translated into 67 languages and broken record after record in both the publishing and the film worlds. Starting with *Harry Potter and the Goblet of Fire*, each successive release smashed the previous record for numbers of books in an initial print run. *Harry Potter and the Deathly Hallows* became the fastest selling book in history, with fifteen million copies sold worldwide in the first 24 hours. Many have tried to explain the phenomenal success of the series, but it almost seems to defy explanation.

We can, however, point to some reasons why the series can touch, enthuse and potentially extend gifted and talented students in particular. The following are some important features that help to explain its value in this area.

In-depth Issues

At its heart, the Harry Potter series has a great story. A surface reading reveals an entertaining story of a quest, a coming-of-age, the triumph of good over evil. But the more you think about it, the more there is to discover. A deeper reading reveals incredible intricacies and complexities (Anelli, 2008). The most obvious themes in the series include concepts such as death, choices, love, power and prejudice. In academic books and journals and at fan conferences and symposiums, complex issues are highlighted and debated. Some examples of thought-provoking investigations (from Baggett & Klein, 2004) are:

- ❖ *All the Minister's Men: Analysing Power and the Press in Harry Potter*
- ❖ *Goblins, Centaurs, House-Elves and Werewolves, Oh My!: The Construction of Otherness and Disability in Harry Potter*
- ❖ *Is the best mum a dead mum? Parenting in the Potterverse*
- ❖ *Feminism and Equal Opportunity: Hermione and the Women of Hogwarts*

So there is plenty of meat here for gifted readers to get their teeth into. Their advanced emotional maturity may mean that they are ready to discuss the types of issues and themes referred to above before other students of the same age. The high fantasy genre, to which Harry Potter belongs, tends to have an inherent appeal to gifted readers, who can see beyond the surface of a story to the spirit contained within (Halstead, 2009). Additionally, well-read students enjoy the sophisticated word-play, the influence of Latin on invented language, and the allusions to existing mythology (Gross et al, 2003).

Role Models

J.K. Rowling herself presents an obvious role model for young gifted girls in particular, clearly demonstrating the importance of resilience. What would have happened if J.K. Rowling had been disheartened when her book was initially rejected by publishers and had given up?

In her characters, students can also find role models with whom they can identify, especially for highly able children. Hermione is the obvious choice, appearing as the typical image of a gifted child, always top of the class, reading text books for fun and answering every question in class. Witness the sometimes negative reactions this behavior engenders from her classmates, and even sometimes, from teachers.

> *"Five more points from Gyffindor for being an insufferable know-it-all."*
> Professor Snape to Hermione
> *Harry Potter and the Prisoner of Azkaban,* Chapter 9

In contrast, Harry is a talented Quidditch player and this sporting giftedness is welcomed and celebrated by his fellow students. While he sometimes struggles with his studies, he demonstrates a natural affinity with Defence Against the Dark Arts and is adept at problem-solving. He also demonstrates strong leadership qualities, a trait that is often associated with gifted students. Other common gifted characteristics can also be seen in Harry, in particular his advanced moral development and his concern with justice and fairness.

Ron represents the invisible or underachieving gifted student. We are given early evidence of his intellectual ability, demonstrated quite ably in his brilliant chess playing skills, but he is not motivated to study like Hermione is and often feels overshadowed by Harry and his older brothers. However, it is Ron, not Harry, who is selected as prefect in his fifth year, so presumably Dumbledore at least spotted his potential. He also displays intense loyalty worthy of a Hufflepuff!

Outside of the books but within the Harry Potter phenomenon, other potential role models emerge. In 1999, Emerson Spartz was a twelve year old homeschooler when he created his own Harry Potter fansite. Mugglenet is now the most popular Harry Potter website on the internet, was visited by more than 25 million people in 2010 and generates over $1 million of revenue each year. By the time he was 17, Emerson had been personally invited by J.K. Rowling to visit Edinburgh and interview her on the day of the release of book six.

A Word about Hufflepuff

Recently, I attended a concert where they were playing several pieces from the Harry Potter score, so they encouraged audience members to come in costume. I'm sure they were only expecting a few kids to come dressed as Harry or Hermione, but as a long-time Harry Potter fan myself, I couldn't resist the opportunity to dress up.

So, when asked which character I was, I had to answer that I was Professor McGonagall, but with a Hufflepuff heart. (I had to be Professor McGonagall because I have the hat!). I also have a shirt which reads 'Hufflepuff and proud.' The 'and proud' bit is important, as if you are familiar with the Harry Potter series, you will know that Hufflepuff gets a bit of a raw deal. Gryffindor have the bravest students, Ravenclaw has the smartest, Slytherin have the most ambitious students, and Hufflepuff? Well, Hufflepuff has 'the rest.' Even well-meaning Hagrid tells us, "Everyone says Hufflepuff are a lot o' duffers."

However, the truth is that Hufflepuff is the growth mindset House. The growth mindset is a belief that intelligence is malleable, and that with effort, anyone can improve their ability in virtually anything (Dweck, 2012). Consider the characteristics that the Sorting Hat looks for in Hufflepuff students:

> *You might belong in Hufflepuff,*
> *Where they are just and loyal,*
> *Those patient Hufflepuffs are true*
> *And unafraid of toil.*
>
> *Harry Potter and the Philosopher's Stone*

Clearly Hufflepuff House values hard work and effort. Students in Hufflepuff know that success doesn't come without effort, they know the value of persistence and they demonstrate resilience and grit in the face of adversity. Unfortunately, in our society of instant gratification, hard work and effort has a bit of a bad name. Malcolm Gladwell, the well-known author who popularized the idea of 'the 10,000 hour rule,' asserts that our society values natural, effortless success over achievement through effort. Carol Dweck, in her important book, Mindset, points out that fables like the Tortoise and the Hare contribute to the negative image of effort, although its intention is the opposite. That story reinforces the idea that effort is for plodders, but in rare instances when those more naturally talented drop the ball, fall over, or fall asleep, the plodder may sneak through and win the race. Not a great message.

This attitude clearly permeates the wizarding world, just as it does among us Muggles. Hufflepuffs rarely get any glory, and they don't stand out as being powerful, valiant or brilliant. They are the quiet achievers, toiling away in the background, and they are derided for it. In the past, I have run Harry Potter workshops for students in which they are divided into groups based on the four Houses of Hogwarts. Those in the Hufflepuff group are often initially disappointed that they weren't assigned to one of the 'cool' Houses. We need to create a climate where hard work and effort is so highly valued that it becomes cool to be a Hufflepuff.

My groups were usually formed randomly, but when students arrive at Hogwarts, the Sorting Hat decides which House they should be placed in, based on the virtues which were prized by the school's founders.

> *Said Slytherin, "We'll teach just those*
> *Whose ancestry is purest."*
> *Said Ravenclaw, "We'll teach those whose*
> *Intelligence is surest."*
> *Said Gryffindor, "We'll teach all those*
> *With brave deeds to their name,"*
> *Said Hufflepuff, "I'll teach the lot,*
> *And treat them just the same."*

> *Harry Potter and the Order of the Phoenix*

It sounds to me like Helga Hufflepuff definitely has a growth mindset. She obviously believes that 11 years old is far too early to tell what a child's future may hold or what talents they may have. Carol Dweck would certainly agree, as she states in her book, "How can we know where effort and time will take someone?" Unfortunately, many times children are 'sorted' even earlier than this. Even Dumbledore expressed regret as he told Snape, "You know, sometimes I think we Sort too soon." We need to be aware of the possible consequences of this and be open to the possibility that students can surprise us and reveal hidden talents at any age.

We need to be sure that we not only nurture talent when it emerges, but always leave the door open for talent to show itself later on, as well as provide plenty of opportunities for our students to discover their own strengths and passions. The challenging activities in this book can help students to do just that.

We also have to make sure our children understand that no matter how much ability you might have, success or achievement does not come without a great deal of hard work and effort. This is especially important for our most highly able students, who may become accustomed to success coming easily, (and if we're not careful, develop the kind of arrogant sense of entitlement more associated with Slytherin).

Additionally, we can give them better role models for effort than the poor beleaguered tortoise. There are plenty of them out there. J.K. Rowling is a great example of the rewards that come after years of dedicated hard work, persistence and resilience. And, not surprisingly, she herself is a Hufflepuff.

Asking students which House they identify with and why can be a great way to start the conversation about which attributes and attitudes are valued in our society and which are likely to lead to success and fulfillment.

Beyond the Books

One of the enduring legacies of the Harry Potter series has been the creativity it has inspired in its fans. The internet is awash with examples of Harry Potter-inspired ingenuity. The popular website fanfiction.net alone contains more than half a million 'fanfics' set in the world of Harry Potter – creative writing inspired by the series. The internet allows today's young readers to more actively engage with their reading material than ever before. Crafting a fanfic allows students to recognize and utilize archetypes and motifs in their own and others' literature and to extend or elaborate on the author's original work (Mathew & Adams, 2009). When they post it online (with appropriate safeguards), they gain a genuine audience for the work and possibly useful feedback from their readers as well.

Readers' interpretation of the work of J.K. Rowling is not limited to the written word. Other responses include fanart, a series of Harry Potter Puppet plays, a full-length Harry Potter Musical (and sequel!) and one very patient fan who made a stop-motion animated version of Deathly Hallows – The Movie, using Lego! The series has also inspired the creation of a new musical genre – Wizard

Rock or Wrock. Bands with names such as 'Harry and the Potters', 'Draco and the Malfoys', and 'Ministry of Magic' sing about events in the books, the power of love, and their assertion that 'Voldemort can't stop the Rock!'

Tapping into students' passions and interests is an important step in supporting students to achieve their academic potential. Research shows that student interest is critical for talent development, as students who are interested in what they are learning are motivated to pursue learning experiences of ever-increasing complexity and difficulty (Powell & Kusuma-Powell, 2011). No doubt the young fan who completed the ambitious stop-motion animation project mentioned above, learned a lot about the art and craft of movie-making, as well as more nebulous skills like persistence, stamina and grit.

J.K. Rowling has long been credited with turning kids on to reading, with encouraging a generation of digital natives to rediscover the joy of a good book, but for James Thomas, an English Professor in the United States, it goes much deeper than that:

> They've made millions of kids smarter, more sensitive, certainly more literate and probably more ethical and aware of hypocrisy and lust for power. They've made children better adults, I think. I don't know of any books that have worked that kind of magic on so many millions of readers in so short a time in the history of publications.
>
> James Thomas, quoted in Gibbs (2007)

Imagine Better

From Wizard Rock came wizard activism. The **Harry Potter Alliance** is a charitable organization that fights the Dark Arts in the real world using the power of Harry Potter. With a catch cry of 'the weapon we have is love,' the HP Alliance uses parallels in the Harry Potter books to educate and mobilise young people around the world towards issues of literacy, equality and human rights. Their manifesto is directly inspired by the words of J.K. Rowling:

> We do not need magic to change the world, we carry all the power we need inside ourselves already: we have the power to imagine better.
>
> J.K. Rowling

Taking inspiration from the wizarding world, the Harry Potter Alliance (HPA) has been responsible for preparing thousands of young student leaders to get involved in civic engagement in their own communities and more widely, and to tackle global issues of confronting genocide, equal rights, environmental protection, media reform, fair trade and literacy.

Service-based learning has the potential to positively affect academic achievement for students of all ability levels. Combining the benefits of service learning with the passion inspired by Harry Potter has the potential to positively impact student learning as well as to create meaningful social change. Students could be encouraged to join their local chapter of the HPA, or perhaps even to start their own. They could start by considering how they might get involved in one of the HPA's campaigns, or how it might be applied to their own community.

The possibilities that the Harry Potter series has for unleashing the creativity and resourcefulness of students are virtually limitless. The activities in this resource guide are just a start to encourage a deeper exploration of J.K. Rowling's wonderful creation.

How to use the activities in this resource

By their very nature, these activities have a strong literacy basis. They are, after all, inspired by a hefty seven-book series which naturally assumes that students will be highly competent readers. As well as extending able students in language arts, most activities address at least one other area of learning such as critical thinking, problem solving or argument and reasoning. The activities also allow you some versatility in the way that you use them, as they can be used in different ways to suit your needs, and can suit a variety of grouping arrangements.

The table on page 16 provides an at-a-glance guide to which areas are addressed by each activity, as well as the grouping arrangements most suitable for it. Some suggestions for the broader context in which you set the activities follow.

Bringing Hogwarts to Life

One of my favourite ways to use these activities is as an immersive enrichment workshop running over one or more days. This could be as part of school-based provision, or an extra-curricular summer camp or similar. This gives you the opportunity to totally immerse the students in the Hogwarts experience.

You can begin by setting the scene with some Harry Potter inspired decorations. Movie or book posters are good, and you might be able to persuade your local cinema or bookshop to give you some. Dressing up also helps to set the mood. You can also insist that students call you 'Professor' for the duration of the workshop.

Everyone knows that new students at Hogwarts need to be Sorted into a House by the Sorting Hat, so this is the first thing you should do at the start of the experience. Unless you have a talking hat handy, you will need to use an ordinary witch's hat (such as those sold around Halloween). Have some slips of paper with the four House names on them in the hat. Students pick one out of the hat and are thus Sorted into their Houses. If you are feeling creative, it can be possible to create a talking 'sorting hat' using an accomplice and a baby monitor, and this might allow more control over which student ends up in which House. There are also many online quizzes which will allocate students to Houses based on their answers to particular questions, but using that method may well result in unevenly sized groups. Being Sorted by the hat usually eliminates any complaints that you might ordinarily get if students are not put into groups with their friends.

You might also make small laminated House ID badges which students can wear to declare their allegiances. Students will then stay in their House groups for the duration of the workshop or camp. Many of the activities have an element of competition and a sense of House unity will soon develop among the students.

House points can be awarded throughout the day. You might give each group a house point jar, into which their house points go as they collect them. I have successfully used jellybeans for house points. Someone will always ask if they are allowed to eat them as they earn them, and I always tell them that they can eat them if they choose, but that will mean they won't be there to be counted at the end of the workshop when the House Championship will be decided. That competitive edge kicks in and the house points are always left untouched! It's a great lesson in delayed gratification. At the end of the workshop the points (jellybeans) are counted and the House champions announced. Then all groups get to share their edible House points between their members. As a non-edible alternative, you could also use buttons or beads or something similar.

If using the activities in this kind of immersive experience, many of them can be re-named to fit the subjects taught at Hogwarts. So the anagram activity becomes Transfiguration, the levitation challenge becomes Charms, and Hagrid's breeding experiment becomes Care of Magical Creatures.

Wizard Withdrawals

For a group of students who are withdrawn from the regular classroom for extension in English, these activities could provide a focus for a term's work, with one or two activities completed each week. If numbers permit, students can still be grouped into Houses to maintain continuity from week to week, although using jellybeans for points may not be such a wise choice over an extended period – buttons or beads could be used instead, or students could create a visual tally system. This kind of arrangement could also work for an after-school enrichment club.

In the Regular Classroom

If you just have a few students in your class in need of extension in literacy, you can still use most, but not all, of these activities. While the rest of the class is working on the regular curriculum, a small group of more able students can work on the extension activities presented here. However, while most of the activities can be worked on by students independently, some input from the teacher, teacher aide or teaching assistant will help to get the most out of them.

Likewise, if you only have one student in your class in need of extension, there are some activities, such as the Learning Ladders, suited to individual independent work. However, if it is possible to find another like-minded student to work on the activities together, it would be preferable. The process of making meaning and developing understanding can be greatly enhanced by the opportunity to share learning experiences and discuss them with peers of similar ability.

Must students be Harry Potter fans to complete these activities?

Clearly Harry Potter fans of all ages will enjoy engaging with the books on a higher level and working on these challenging complementary activities. But what if you have some highly able students in your class who are not yet fully fledged Harry Potter fans – can you still use these activities with them?

The answer is, in some cases, yes. An in-depth knowledge of the world of Harry Potter is a prerequisite for some, but not all, of these activities. If you have students who have seen some of the movies but not yet read the books, they may still be able to participate in some of these activities. Hopefully, their participation will inspire them to go on and read the books for themselves. If so, it can be useful to ask them to complete the Learning Ladder tasks specific to the book they are reading, as an independent learning project during in-class literacy times, so that they extend their understanding as they go.

Activity Overview

ACTIVITY	FOCUS AREA(S)	GROUPING ARRANGEMENT
Investigating potions	Science, problem solving	Small groups
The hero's journey	Language arts (writing), critical thinking	Individual, pairs, small groups
Anagrams never lie	Language arts (reading), problem solving	Individual, pairs, small groups
What's in a name?	Language arts (reading), creative thinking	Individual, pairs, small groups
How well can you spell?	Language arts (reading), creative thinking	Individual, pairs, small groups
What's your boggart?	Drama, critical thinking	Large group
Hagrid's experimental breeding program	Visual art, creative thinking	Individual, pairs
A potty perspective	Language arts (writing)	Individual
Ordinary Wizarding Levels	Creative thinking	Pairs, small groups
Wingardium Leviosa (the levitation challenge)	Creative thinking, problem solving	Small groups
Literary lifeboat	Language arts (speaking & listening), argument, reason	Large group
Hogwarts staff meeting	Language arts (speaking & listening), argument, reason	Small groups, large group
Dynamic discussion	Language arts (speaking & listening), critical thinking	Small groups, large group
Riddikulus riddles	Language arts, critical & creative thinking	Pairs, small groups
Wizard wordplay	Language arts (writing), critical & creative thinking	Individual, pairs, small groups
Learning ladders	Multiple	Individual, pairs, small groups, large group

Investigating Potions

In this two-stage activity, students work with 'magic potions' to explore the properties of bases and acids.

Focus areas   Science, problem-solving

Organisation   Students should work cooperatively in their house groups

Resources   Red cabbage
Water
Baking soda
White vinegar
Lemonade (or any of the carbonated lemon soft drinks that go under a brand name)
Ammonia (clear if you can get it, but cloudy will do)
4 small clear bottles
20 clear plastic cups
One copy of the **Revealing Riddle** for each group
One copy of the pH scale for each student

Preparation

1.   A day or two before carrying out the activity, (no earlier), prepare the Revealing Solution. To do this, chop some of the red cabbage, put it in a saucepan with some water and boil it for as long as you can stand the smell – 20 to 30 minutes will do. Let it cool, then strain off the liquid and divide it between the four small bottles. If you're feeling especially creative, make a label for each of the bottles. You can use the provided template, or make one of your own.

2.   Prepare the plastic cups. You will need one set of five cups for each group, clearly labeled: A, B, C, D and E.

3.   Prepare a set of potion name cards for each group. A piece of folded card works well. The potions are as follows:

Shrinking Solution   Draught of Living Death   Veritaserum
Ageing Potion   Essence of Gillyweed

Revealing Potion: Sample label

Hector Dagworth Granger's
Revealing Solution
Most Extraordinary Society of Potioneers

What to do
STAGE 1

1. Explain that the students will be investigating the properties of potions and identifying five different potions whose labels have got mixed up.
2. For each group, prepare five clear cups each containing a little of each of the following solutions: plain water; a solution of baking soda and water; white vinegar; lemonade; and ammonia (refer to the table below for details). Don't let the students see you doing this!
3. Give each group a copy of the Potions Riddle, a set of potions labels, and a bottle of Revealing Solution.
4. Instruct them to add a couple of drops of Revealing Solution to each potion and to use the Riddle and the results to correctly identify each potion.

The potions and their properties

LABEL	POTION	SUBSTANCE	COLOUR	ACID/BASE
A	Shrinking Solution	Ammonia	Green	Base
B	Ageing Potion	Baking soda solution	Blue	Base
C	Veritaserum	Plain water	Purple	Acid
D	Draught of Living Death	White vinegar	Red	Acid
E	Essence of Gillyweed	Lemonade	Pink	Acid

! Alert ! Instruct students *not* to drink the potions

STAGE 2

1. Once all groups have correctly identified all five potions, ask if anyone can identify which scientific concept the activity demonstrates. Depending on the age and prior knowledge of the students, they may be able to recognise that the activity demonstrate acids and bases.

2. Provide all students with some background information on acids and bases and a pH scale. Some basic information is provided here, but you may like to elaborate on this depending on the students' existing knowledge and your own familiarity with this topic.

3. Provide students with the identity of the real ingredients and present them with the following challenges:

   o   Can you work out which of the potions are acids and which are bases?
   o   Now you have this information, can you identify what substances were actually in the cups?
   o   Using your knowledge of acids and bases, choose one of the potions and write a recipe for it. You should use a combination of real and magical ingredients, and choose acidic or basic ingredients as appropriate.

Background Information

Every liquid you see will probably either be an acid or a base. One exception is distilled water. The positive and negative ions in distilled water are in equal amounts and cancel each other out. Most tap water has ions in it, which is why the water in our experiment is slightly acidic. It is the ions in a solution that make something acidic or basic. Fruits contain something called citric acid. Vinegar is another acid. But when baking soda is dissolved in water, it creates a basic solution.

Scientists use the **pH scale** to express how acidic (like an acid) or basic (like a base) a substance is.

   ❖   A pH value below 7 means that a substance is acidic; the smaller the number, the more acidic it is.
   ❖   A pH value above 7 means that a substance is basic; the larger the number, the more basic it is.
   ❖   A pH value of 7 is neutral

Adding red cabbage extract to a substance can indicate whether it is an acid (like vinegar) or a base (like ammonia). It can also show how strong an acid or a base a substance is. Red cabbage has this capacity because it contains water-soluble pigments called **anthocyanins** which change colour according to whether they are in the presence of an acid or an alkali. The red cabbage extract will turn a particular colour according to the pH value of the substance, as illustrated in the table below.

Colour of red cabbage extract along the pH scale

Approximate pH	2	4	6	8	10	12
Colour of extract	Red	Purple	Violet	Blue	Blue-green	Green

The pH scale goes from values very close to 0 up to 14. Distilled water is 7 (right in the middle). Acids are found between 0 and 7. Bases are from 7 to 14. Most of the common liquids we come into contact with have a pH near 7. It is when you start looking at the pH of chemicals that the numbers go to the extremes of 1 and 14. There are also very strong acids with pH values below one such as battery acid. Bases with pH values near 14 include drain cleaner and sodium hydroxide (NaOH). Those chemicals are very dangerous.

pH scale

pH	1	2	3	4	5	6	7	8	9	10	11	12	13	14
Type	Acids						Neutral							Bases
Colour	Dark red	Light red	Dark orange	Light orange	Dark yellow	Light yellow	Light green	Dark green	Light blue	mid blue	Dark blue	purple	Light purple	violet
Example	Battery acid						Distilled water					Drain cleaner		

Revealing Riddle

If the truth is what you seek,
Then don't choose pink, it is too weak.
For a tongue you seek to loosen,
Red is not the colour of the solution.

If underwater action is your goal,
The red potion will leave you cold.
Green will leave you feeling small,
It's not the one you want at all.

Asphodel and wormwood together will keep
The drinker in the deepest sleep.
The Draught you seek will turn a hue,
But it won't be purple and it won't be blue.

If something you wish to shrink,
Then don't choose red and don't choose pink.
Red will not cause you to age,
Nor will purple, and nor will sage.

Blue might make you grow a beard.
Pink might leave you feeling weird.
Make your choice but heed the clues.
You must be careful which you choose.

Harry Potter and the Hero's Journey

> This activity introduces the powerful concept of the hero's journey to develop a deeper understanding of Harry Potter's story and to indicate how it can be applied more widely in literature and film.

Focus areas	Language arts (writing), critical thinking
Organisation	Students can work individually, in pairs, or in small groups
Resources	One copy of the resource sheet, **Identifying the hero's journey** in *Harry Potter and the Philosopher's Stone* for each student, pair or group.

What to do

1. Introduce the topic of this activity with a whole group discussion:

   o Ask students if they can identify any similarities between Harry Potter's journey and those of other fictional heroes from books or movies. Discuss any examples they suggest, such as Frodo from Lord of the Rings or Luke Skywalker from Star Wars.

   o Explain the concept of the Hero's Journey, as described by Joseph Campbell and Christopher Vogler (see background information).

   o Explain and discuss each stage of the Hero's Journey, seeking lots of examples from popular culture, literature and movies.

2. As a whole group, consider and discuss *Harry Potter and the Philosopher's Stone* in terms of the Hero's Journey. Try to find an example for each stage from the book. Some suggestions are provided, but these are open to individual interpretation. Students can use the resource sheet to note down the group-generated suggestions, or a master record can be made on an interactive whiteboard or similar.

3. Ask students, preferably in pairs or small groups, to consider one other book in the Harry Potter series and complete the exercise, finding an example for each stage from their chosen book.

4. As a whole group, share and discuss each group's responses. Ensure students recognise that while elements of the Hero's Journey can be seen in each volume of the Harry Potter series, the model can also be applied to the series as a whole.

5. You could discuss whether J.K. Rowling consciously used the hero's journey template to guide her writing, or whether the story just naturally evolved to follow that pattern. After all, early myths such as those of Hercules or Achilles certainly were not written to a formula, but they still follow a common pattern. Within the Harry Potter novels, certain elements appear to emerge very strongly, such as the way the story always begins in the Ordinary World. Stage 7, 'Approaching the innermost cave', was traditionally a descent into the underworld or an entry into the land of the dead. Consider the location of the climactic scenes in at least the first five Harry Potter novels:

   o in *Philosopher's Stone*, Harry goes through the trapdoor and descends into a hidden area
   o in *Chamber of Secrets*, the climax takes place in a hidden chamber deep under the school
   o in *Prisoner of Azkaban*, the protagonists enter an underground tunnel which leads to the Shrieking Shack
   o *Goblet of Fire* stays above ground, but in a graveyard, definitely a land of the dead
   o *Order of the Phoenix* descends into the bowels of the Ministry of Magic, again underground.

The final two novels deviate from this pattern, with the action taking place on top of the astronomy tower, and in the Hogwarts grounds and forest. Students may like to discuss these patterns and their impact, or possible reasons for altering the established pattern.

Possible extension activity: Students could use the hero's journey model to develop their own work of fiction.

Background Information

Joseph Campbell was an American mythologist who studied myths and legends from around the world. He recognised that they followed a familiar pattern, which he described as the **hero's journey**. Later, Christopher Vogler took Campbell's hero's journey structure and revised it, simplifying it a little and referring to it as the **writer's journey**.

The best known and best remembered stories follow this pattern, from ancient myths through to more modern day fables including, of course, the Harry Potter series. The steps on the following page are those described by Vogler (1992), presenting a more useful and user-friendly model to use with students than Campbell's original version.

After reading through the activity, discuss how the hero's journey applies to the examples listed below. Add any others students can think of, with the exception of the Harry Potter series, which is the main focus of this activity.

Examples of the hero's journey

STORY	HERO	ELEMENTS OF THE HERO'S JOURNEY
The Labours of Hercules	Hercules	
The Odyssey	Odysseus	
The Iliad	Achilles	
The Legends of King Arthur	Arthur Pendragon	
The Lord of the Rings	Frodo Baggins	
The Adventures of Robin Hood	Robin Hood	
The Lion King	Simba	
Star Wars IV – VI	Luke Skywalker	

Overview of the hero's journey

1. Ordinary World: The story starts in the ordinary world with the hero going about their everyday existence, oblivious of the adventures to come. This anchors the hero as a human, just like you and me, which helps us to identify with the hero.

2. Call to Adventure: Something shakes up the situation, from either external or internal pressures. The hero must face the beginnings of change.

3. Refusal of the Call: The hero feels the fear of the unknown and tries to turn away from the adventure, however briefly. Alternately, another character may express the uncertainty and danger ahead.

4. Meeting the Mentor: The mentor appears to help the hero prepare for the road ahead. Thus Gandalf, Obi-wan Kenobi, Dumbledore or other wise and experienced people teach the hero the skills they need and give them essential knowledge to help them survive.

5. Crossing the Threshold: Eventually the hero is ready to act and crosses the threshold, often literally, as they leave the safety of home to begin their journey into the unknown.

6. Tests, Allies, Enemies: The hero is confronted with an ever more difficult series of challenges, ranging from minor skirmishes and struggles against weather and terrain to riddles and various setbacks that would defeat a lesser person. In this way the hero's character is both highlighted and developed.

7. Approaching the Innermost Cave: The hero approaches the final destination, battered but wiser from their trials along the way. They must prepare for the ultimate test. In ancient legend, a typical 'innermost cave' is the land of the dead or a labyrinth. It is the lair of the dreaded enemy where no help may be found and only deep courage will win through. Another threshold must be crossed here to enter the innermost cave.

8. Ordeal: At last the hero must face their deepest fears, typically in battle with the dark villain. This is the ultimate test that the hero takes, where the real story perhaps is the inner battle whereby the hero overcomes their own demons in facing up to the enemy outside.

9. Reward (seizing the sword): In defeating the enemy, the hero is transformed into a new state where fears are vanquished and the new fearless person is born. The reward in the story may be gaining new knowledge, a treasure or rescuing a princess, but the inner reward is in the personal growth that is achieved.

10. The Road Back: After the story has reached its main peak, the transformed hero sets out for home again. Having gained the treasure they have no need for more adventure and nothing left to prove. Setting out home is a reverse echo of crossing the threshold in the beginning of the adventure. In contrast to the earlier anticipation of danger, the anticipation now is of acclaim and rest.

11. Resurrection: The story has one last trick up its sleeve. Having lulled its audience into a false sense of security, one last challenge faces the hero. Perhaps the villain was not completely vanquished or perhaps there are other people in need on the way back -- whichever way, we are again plunged into another climactic event, just when we thought it was safe to breathe easy again.

12. Return with the Elixir: Finally, the hero returns to the hero's welcome, gives the treasure to the proper recipient and receives their just reward, whether it is the hand of the princess, the acclaim of the people or simply a well-deserved rest. In this final part, all tensions are resolved and all unanswered questions answered, leaving the reader of the story satisfied and replete.

Source: Adapted from Vogler (1992)

Resource sheet: Identifying the hero's journey in *Harry Potter and the Philosopher's Stone*

STAGE OF THE JOURNEY	EXAMPLE(S) FROM THE BOOK
Ordinary world	
Call to adventure	
Refusal of the call	
Meeting the mentor	
Crossing the threshold	
Tests, allies, enemies	
Approaching the innermost cave	
Ordeal	
Reward (seizing the sword)	
The road back	
Resurrection	
Return with the elixir	

Sample Answers
Resource sheet: Identifying the hero's journey in *Harry Potter and the Philosopher's Stone*

STAGE OF THE JOURNEY	EXAMPLE(S) FROM THE BOOK
Ordinary world	*4 Privet Drive, life with the Dursleys*
Call to adventure	*The letters start to arrive*
Refusal of the call	*Here it's not Harry who is refusing but Vernon, who does everything he can to stop Harry getting the letters*
Meeting the mentor	*The main mentor in the series is Dumbledore, but he sometimes acts through others. Here it's Hagrid at the Hut on the Rock*
Crossing the threshold	*The physical threshold at Kings Cross. Also the magical threshold into Diagon Alley.*
Tests, allies, enemies	*Tests – troll, Norbert, Quidditch* *Allies – Ron & Hermione* *Enemies – Malfoy & Snape*
Approaching the innermost cave	*Descending through the trapdoor and navigating the series of challenges guarding the stone*
Ordeal	*Facing Professor Quirrel and Voldemort (in the back of Quirrel's head!)*
Reward (seizing the sword)	*Obtaining the Philosopher's Stone*
The road back	*Waking up in the hospital wing. Debriefing with Dumbledore*
Resurrection	*We learn the danger is not past, Voldemort will return*
Return with the elixir	*Harry (and friends) receive enough House Points to win the House Cup for Gryffindor*

Anagrams Never Lie

Focus areas	Language Arts (reading), problem-solving
Organisation	This activity works well with a group, with an element of competition, but could also be done individually.
Resources	One copy of the resource sheet, **Decoding anagrams**, for each student Copies of the **cheat sheet** (optional)

Recommended anagram websites

Internet Anagram Server	www.wordsmith.org/anagram
Anagram Genius	www.anagramgenius.com

TOM MARVOLO RIDDLE becomes I AM LORD VOLDEMORT

With this example revealed in *Chamber of Secrets*, J.K. Rowling herself opened up the never-ending possibilities of hidden meanings within the books. While fans of the series eagerly waited for each new installment, fan-sites on the internet were a hive of activity with discussion of theories about what might happen next and what seemingly fleeting incident might be a clue to future storylines. For example, when Neville visits his parents in the closed ward at St. Mungo's, his mother presses a Droobles Best Blowing Gum wrapper into his hand. Rearranging the letters in *'Droobles Best Blowing Gum'* gives you *'Gold bribe below St. Mungo's'* which led to a complicated theory suggesting that Neville's parents weren't really insane but were being deliberately kept in that state by some evil plot! That idea turned out to be incorrect, but it was a lot of fun speculating.

Answers:
1. OLLIVANDER, 2. HARRY POTTER, 3. EMMELINE VANCE, 4. ALBUS DUMBLEDORE,
5. DOLORES JANE UMBRIDGE, 6. SEVERUS SNAPE, 7. PETER PETTIGREW,
8. ARTHUR WEASLEY, 9. DEAN THOMAS, 10. NYMPHADORA TONKS

What to do

1. Discuss J.K. Rowling's use of anagrams and other plays on words in the Harry Potter series. Even in the first book, there are hints at deeper meanings with the Mirror of Erised and in the geographical names Diagon Alley and Knockturn Alley. (Have students noticed what is special about each of these three examples?) The resource sheet, **Decoding anagrams**, provides some additional examples you could discuss as a group.

2. Hand out copies of the resource sheet and challenge the students to solve the anagrams on it. To introduce an element of competition, set individuals or groups the challenge of being the first to solve all 10 anagrams.

   Students may need a reminder of some lesser-known characters in order to solve all of the anagrams. After the students have solved as many as possible on their own, you may choose to give them the Cheat Sheet which lists all 10 solutions among a longer list of possible answers.

   After solving the anagrams, students may like to share their successful strategies.

3. Can students think of any other examples of books, games or movies where anagrams are used? Possible examples could be the *Deltora Quest* books and *The Da Vinci Code* book and movie.

4. Challenge students to make an anagram using their own name. Can they make any words or phrases? Students might use an internet anagram server to help with suggestions. Imagine my surprise to discover that my name anagrams to Her Legal Lasagne!

5. As a variation on the above, students can rearrange the letters in their name to make an alias – perhaps a more wizardy sounding name that could be used as a character in a fantasy story. My wizardy anagram name is Helga Sallagreen.

Resource sheet: Decoding anagrams

Here are some examples of anagrams connected to the Harry Potter books:

TOM MARVOLO RIDDLE becomes **I AM LORD VOLDEMORT**

Think about what happens in the first chapter of Goblet of Fire. Is it any wonder that the chapter title is an anagram?

THE RIDDLE HOUSE becomes **THREE SHOULD DIE**

And how's this for spooky? The director of the fourth film was Mike Newell, so it could be referred to as:

MIKE NEWELL'S HARRY POTTER AND THE GOBLET OF FIRE

which becomes

ENTHRALLING FILM, YET WE PREFER TO READ THE BOOKS

Listed below are some anagrams formed from characters' names. In most cases the anagram also provides a clue to the character's identity. See how many you can solve.

1. AN EVIL LORD

2. TRY HERO PART

3. EVIL MEN MENACE

4. BLAMED OLD RUBEUS

5. DUMBLEDORE GOES IN JAR

6. SAVE PURENESS

7. TIP: PET WE REGRET

8. WE SALUTE HARRY

9. MAN SO HATED

10. ON HAND TO MARK SPY

CHEAT SHEET for Resource Sheet: Decoding anagrams

The anagrams match 10 of the characters named here:

HARRY POTTER	ALBUS DUMBLEDORE
RUBEUS HAGRID	ARTHUR WEASLEY
RON WEASLEY	MINERVA MCGONAGALL
PETER PETTIGREW	MOLLY WEASLEY
HERMIONE GRANGER	SEVERUS SNAPE
NYMPHADORA TONKS	BARTEMIUS CROUCH
SEAMUS FINNIGAN	REMUS LUPIN
KINGSLEY SHACKLEBOLT	FLOREAN FORTESCUE
DEAN THOMAS	LUDO BAGMAN
EMMELINE VANCE	OLLIVANDER
NEVILLE LONGBOTTOM	RITA SKEETER
DOLORES JANE UMBRIDGE	DEDALUS DIGGLE

What's in a Name?

J.K. Rowling has chosen her character names with great care. In many cases, the name gives the reader clues about a character's traits or role within the series. Here is an opportunity for students to recognise these links and explore them more closely.

Focus areas   Language arts (reading), creative thinking

Organisation   Students can work individually, in pairs or in small groups

Resources   One copy of the resource sheet, **A new middle name**, for each student
Selection of mythology books
Latin dictionary
Good English dictionaries and thesauruses

What to do

1. Discuss with students some of the character names from the Harry Potter series. Can they explain the meaning behind some of the names? Some are discussed on the resource sheet, but the following are others the students may be aware of:

NAME	ASSOCIATIONS
Albus	White
Hermes (Percy's owl)	Greek god, messenger to Zeus
Argus (Filch)	From Greek mythology, giant with 100 eyes
Lucius (Malfoy)	Associated with Lucifer or Satan
Narcissa (Malfoy)	From Greek mythology, Narcissus fell in love with his own reflection; narcissistic

2. Hand out copies of the resource sheet, **A new middle name**, and discuss the character names that are listed there.

3. Based on what they know about the characters, students should choose a new middle name for each of the characters listed. They can use the resource books provided for inspiration.

4. Students can share and justify their choices with each other.

Resource sheet: A new middle name

Here are some examples of character names and their possible meanings. Using what you know about each character, create a new middle name to suit them.

~ SIRIUS BLACK ~

The star, Sirius, (also known as the Dog Star) is the brightest star in the sky. Celestial names seem to have been a tradition in the Black household – many others in the family, including Regulus and Andromeda are also named after constellations.

The colour black, which has many associations.

~ REMUS LUPIN ~

From Roman mythology, Remus was raised by a she-wolf, along with his twin brother Romulus. The twin element may also refer to Lupin's dual nature; he is both man and wolf.

The Latin *lupus* which means 'wolf.' A person who looks wolf-like is said to be *lupine*.

~ MINERVA MCGONAGALL ~

Minerva is the Roman goddess of Wisdom.

This Scottish name comes from the Celtic *conegal* which means 'the bravest.'

~ LUDO BAGMAN ~

The Latin word *ludo* means 'I play.'

A bagman collects money for racketeers or is a travelling salesman.

~ DRACO MALFOY ~

Draco is Latin for 'dragon.'

Mal is the Latin root for 'bad' – think about *malevolent* or *malignant*. In French, *mal foi* means 'bad faith.'

FIRST NAME	NEW MIDDLE NAME	FAMILY NAME
Sirius		Black
Remus		Lupin
Minerva		McGonagall
Ludo		Bagman
Draco		Malfoy

How Well Can You Spell?

As with her character names, J.K. Rowling has created magic words for her spells with great care and skill. If Harry had had even the most basic grounding in Latin, there is no way he would have used *Sectumsempra* on Draco Malfoy in the bathroom in *Half Blood Prince*. Many, but not all, of the spells in the series have their roots in Latin, as students will discover through completing this activity.

Focus areas   Language arts (reading), creative thinking

Organisation   Students can work individually, in pairs or in small groups

Resources   One copy of the resource sheet, **Some spells and their etymology**, for each student
Latin (plus possibly Spanish and Italian) dictionaries
Good English dictionaries and thesauruses

What to do

1. Give out copies of the resource sheet, **Some spells and their etymology**, and discuss the examples of spells and their etymologies that it lists. How many are they already aware of?

2. Challenge students to create three (or more) original spells. They should provide the magic word, clearly describe what the spell does, and explain the etymology of the spell. Provide a selection of Latin dictionaries for students to browse through for inspiration. Italian or Spanish dictionaries may also be helpful if you can't find a Latin dictionary or if you only have one and a larger group of students. Good English dictionaries are also invaluable.

Possible extension: Students could write a short vignette in which a Harry Potter character uses one or more of the students' invented spells.

Resource sheet: Some spells and their etymology

MAGIC WORD	PURPOSE OF SPELL	ETYMOLOGY OF MAGIC WORD
Accio	Summoning charm	Means 'to send for' or 'to summon' in Latin
Alohomora	Open locks	Derived from the Hawaiian word *aloha*, meaning 'goodbye' (as well as hello), and the Latin word *mora*, meaning 'obstacle.' So literally, 'goodbye obstacle.'
Crucio	Torture	Latin for 'I torture.' Think about the word *excruciating*.
Expecto patronum	Banish Dementors	In Latin, *expecto* is 'to await, desire or hope for' and *patronus* means 'protector.'
Incendio	Create fire	From the Latin *incendere*, which means 'to set fire to.' *Incendio* is also Spanish for 'great fire.' Think about the word *incendiary*.
Levicorpus (*Liberacorpus* counter-curse)	Suspend someone in mid-air; counter-curse reverses spell	In Latin *levi* means 'to raise' and *corpus* means 'body. *Libera* is Latin for 'to free.' Think about *levitate* and *liberate*.
Lumos	Light up the end of the wand	Derived from *lumen*, which is Latin for 'light.' Think about *illuminate* and *luminous*.
Obliviate	Erase someone's memory	Possibly a combination of the words *obliterate*, which means to wipe out, erase or remove all traces, and *oblivious* meaning forgetful or unaware.
Sectumsempra	Cause serious wounds	In Latin, *sectum* means 'to cut, wound or amputate' and *sempra* is derived from *semper*, meaning 'always, at all times.'

Now write three spells of your own in the table below.

MAGIC WORD	PURPOSE OF SPELL	ETYMOLOGY (to explain your choice)

What's your Boggart?

In the Harry Potter world, a Boggart is a shapeshifting magical creature that takes on the form of whatever will scare the person the most. This activity is based around the traditional dramatic game of charades, with the students taking turns to act out various fears. Most of these are typical fears that might be found among the students at Hogwarts, such as the fear of Dementors or werewolves, but some are common to the Muggle world, such as the fear of heights, or rats.

Focus areas	Drama, critical thinking
Organisation	Students work in a larger group divided into at least two teams.
Resources	A set of **Boggart Cards**, cut out individually A timer – large egg timer or similar

What to do

1. Organise the students into teams, or houses, for the game. Then follow these steps:
   o A student from one team chooses a Boggart card at random from the pile and acts out whatever Boggart is on the card. The usual rules of charades apply, in that students may not speak, but must rely on their miming skills.
   o With the timer set, the student's own team has up to one minute to correctly identify the Boggart. No other team can guess during the first minute.
   o If the student's team cannot guess the Boggart during the first minute, the student continues to mime, but any team can now guess. The team that correctly guesses the Boggart gets a point.
   o The game continues in this way, with teams taking turns to act out the Boggarts, and all students having a turn.
2. Following the game, lead the students in a group discussion about the nature of fear. You could consider questions such as:
   o Does all fear have a physical appearance?
   o What shape would the Boggart take on to represent a fear of the unknown, or the fear of not being perfect?
   o Lupin said that what Harry feared was fear itself, and that this was wise. What did he mean?

Possible extension: Students could write a personal journal entry describing their own fears. They may choose whether or not to share it with the teacher.

Boggart Cards

Use the suggestions here to create a set of Boggart Cards. You could also create some additional ones of your own.

Mummy	Vampire	Centaur
Giants	Professor Snape	Pixies
Dragon	Death Eater	Werewolf
Heights	Thestrals	Banshee
Clowns	Basilisk	Blast-ended Skrewts
The Grim	Voldemort	Dementors
Acromantula	Rats	Failure

Hagrid's Experimental Breeding Program

> **"I can certainly see why we're trying to keep them alive. Who wouldn't want pets that can burn, sting and bite all at once?"**
>
> Draco Malfoy
> *Harry Potter and the Goblet of Fire*, Chapter 13
>
> Who could forget the Blast-Ended Skrewts? These were the result of Hagrid's breeding experiment and were a cross between Manticores and Fire-Crabs. The result was a ferocious, ugly creature that almost defies description – a kind of cross between a giant scorpion and an elongated crab that, as Draco pointed out, could burn, sting and bite all at once.
>
> The premise behind this activity is that Hagrid has not been put off by his first attempt at creating a new species, but is determined to try again.

Focus areas	Visual arts, creative thinking
Organisation	Students can work individually, or in pairs
Resources	Copies of the **Creature cards**, cut out individually or copies of *Fantastic Beasts and Where to Find Them* Art supplies

What to do

1. Discuss the Blast-Ended Skrewt example with the students and explain that their job is to help Hagrid create a new species of magical creature.

2. Read and discuss the creature descriptions on the Creature Cards. Some of these magical creatures feature in the Harry Potter books, but some of them can only be found in J.K. Rowling's companion book, *Fantastic Beasts and Where to Find Them*.

3. Students are to choose two, or a maximum of three different creatures to virtually interbreed. They will create a new species of magical creature. They are to create

a visual representation of their creature. This could be drawn, painted or created using any other artistic technique of your choice, for which you have the necessary supplies.

4. In addition to their picture, students should supply the following information about their creature:

   ❖ The name of the new species

   ❖ The creatures that have been combined to create it

   ❖ A description of its appearance

   ❖ Its eating habits, diet etc.

   ❖ Its sleeping habits

   ❖ Its behaviour

   ❖ Any other relevant information

Possible extension activity: Students could have a go at writing an entry for their creature in the style of *Fantastic Beasts and Where to Find Them.*

CRUP

The Crup originated in the southeast of England. It closely resembles a Jack Russell terrier, except for the forked tail. The Crup is almost certainly a wizard-created dog, as it is intensely loyal to wizards and ferocious towards Muggles. It is a great scavenger, eating anything from gnomes to old tyres. Crup licences may be obtained from the Department for the Regulation and Control of Magical Creatures on completion of a simple test to prove that the applicant wizard is capable of controlling the Crup in Muggle-inhabited areas. Crup owners are legally obliged to remove the Crup's tail with a painless Severing Charm while the Crup is six to eight weeks old, lest Muggles notice it.

DIRICAWL

The Diricawl originated in Mauritius. A plump-bodied, fluffy-feathered, flightless bird, the Diricawl is remarkable for its method of escaping danger. It can vanish in a puff of feathers and reappear elsewhere (the phoenix shares this ability). Interestingly, Muggles were once fully aware of the existence of the Diricawl, though they knew it by the name of 'dodo'. Unaware that the Diricawl could vanish at will, Muggles believe they have hunted the species to extinction. As this seems to have raised Muggle awareness of the dangers of slaying their fellow creatures indiscriminately, the International Confederation of Wizards has never deemed it appropriate that the Muggles should be made aware of the continued existence of the Diricawl.

KNEAZLE

The Kneazle was originally bred in Britain, though it is now exported worldwide. A small cat-like creature with flecked, speckled or spotted fur, outsize ears and a tail like a lion's, the Kneazle is intelligent, independent and occasionally aggressive, though if it takes a liking to a witch or wizard, it makes an excellent pet. The Kneazle has an uncanny ability to detect unsavoury or suspicious characters and can be relied upon to guide its owner safely home if they are lost. Kneazles have up to eight kittens in a litter and can interbreed with cats. Licences are required for ownership as (like Crups and Fwoopers) Kneazles are sufficiently unusual in appearance to attract Muggle interest.

FWOOPER

The Fwooper is an African bird with extremely vivid plumage; Fwoopers may be orange, pink, lime green or yellow. The Fwooper has long been a provider of fancy quills and also lays brilliantly patterned eggs. Though at first enjoyable, Fwooper song will eventually drive the listener to insanity* and the Fwooper is consequently sold with a Silencing Charm upon it, which will need monthly reinforcement. Fwooper owners require licences, as the creatures must be handled responsibly.

*Uric the Oddball attempted at one time to prove that Fwooper song was actually beneficial to the health and listened to it for three months on end without a break. Unfortunately, the Wizards' Council to which he reported his findings were unconvinced, as he had arrived at the meeting wearing nothing but a toupee that on closer inspection proved to be a dead badger.

Source: Fantastic Beasts and Where to Find Them © J.K. Rowling 2001

NIFFLER

The Niffler is a British beast. Fluffy, black and long-snouted, this burrowing creature has a predilection for anything glittery. Nifflers are often kept by goblins to burrow deep into the earth for treasure. Though the Niffler is gentle and even affectionate, it can be destructive to belongings and should never be kept in a house. Nifflers live in lairs up to twenty feet below the surface and produce six to eight young in a litter.

DOXY

The Doxy is often mistaken for a fairy though it is a quite separate species. Like the fairy, it has a minute human form, though in the Doxy's case this is covered in thick black hair and has an extra pair of arms and legs. The Doxy's wings are thick, curved and shiny, much like a beetle's. Doxies are found throughout Northern Europe and America, preferring cold climates. They lay up to five hundred eggs at a time and bury them. The eggs hatch in two to three weeks. Doxies have double rows of sharp, venomous teeth. An antidote should be taken if bitten.

CLABBERT

The Clabbert is a tree-dwelling creature, in appearance something like a cross between a monkey and a frog. It originated in the southern states of America, though it has since been exported worldwide. The smooth and hairless skin is a mottled green, the hands and feet are webbed, and the arms and legs are long and supple, enabling the Clabbert to swing between branches with the agility of an orang-utan. The head has short horns and the wide mouth, which appears to be grinning, is full of razor-sharp teeth. The Clabbert feeds mostly on small lizards and birds.

The Clabbert's most distinctive feature is the large pustule in the middle of its forehead, which turns scarlet and flashes when it senses danger. American wizards once kept Clabberts in their gardens to give early warning of approaching Muggles, but the International Confederation of Wizards has introduced fines which have largely ended this practice. The sight of a tree at night full of glowing Clabbert pustules, while decorative, attracted too many Muggles wishing to ask why their neighbours still had their Christmas lights up in June.

PUFFSKEIN

The Puffskein is found worldwide. Spherical in shape and covered in soft, custard-coloured fur, it is a docile creature that has no objection to being cuddled or thrown about. Easy to care for, it emits a low humming noise when contented. From time to time a very long, thin, pink tongue will emerge from the depths of the Puffskein and snake through the house searching for food. The puffskein is a scavenger that will eat anything from leftovers to spiders, but it has a particular preference for sticking its tongue up the nose of sleeping wizards and eating their bogies. This tendency has made the Puffskein much beloved by wizarding children for many generations and it remains a highly popular wizarding pet.

Source: Fantastic Beasts and Where to Find Them © J.K. Rowling 2001

A Potty Perspective

Focus areas   Language arts (writing)

Organisation   Students work individually

Resources   Copies of the Harry Potter books
Copies of the **Scenario information notes** – the number required will depend on the approach you take with this activity (see below)
Copies of the **Rewriting activity guidelines**

"D'you get the feeling Hermione's not telling us something?" Ron asked Harry.
Harry Potter and the Prisoner of Azkaban, Chapter 7

J.K. Rowling is a master of the red herring, the surprise twist and the unexpected ending. She is able to keep us guessing throughout the series, in large part because of the **narrative voice** that she uses to tell the story. With the exception of the first chapters of *Goblet of Fire, Half-Blood Prince* and *Deathly Hallows*, the story is told from Harry's perspective. As a reader, for the most part, we only know what Harry knows, and sometimes, that's not much! However, the story is not written in the first person, and this gives us a slightly wider perspective than if we were limited to Harry's narration.

The narrative voice J.K. Rowling uses is a variation of third person, called **limited omniscient.** This voice helps us to feel emotionally connected to Harry, but still allows the author to maintain the air of mystery necessary to keep readers guessing.

For this activity, students will experiment with the effect of perspective by rewriting scenes from the book from the perspective of another character.

What to do

1. Discuss with students the effect of using different perspectives. Compare the effects of using the first person and the third person in particular.

2. The approach you choose to take to the rewriting activity may depend on the size and ability level of the group you are working with. For example, you might:

   o Select one of the scenarios and jointly construct a text as a group, before students choose a different scenario to work on independently

   o Ask all the students to independently work on the same scenario, then come together to share their versions and discuss tips and strategies, before choosing a different scenario to work on individually

   o Ask all of the students to work on a scenario of their own choice, initially choosing from one of those provided, before moving on to a self-selected piece of their own.

3. According to the approach you have chosen, students rewrite one of the scenarios from the selection provided (referring to the Harry Potter books for further details) from the different perspective indicated. Discuss the **Rewriting activity guidelines.** Hand out copies for students to refer to and use for planning their rewritten version.

Rewriting activity guidelines

❖ You may choose to write in first person or third person, but it must be from the perspective of the specified character.

❖ Only write about what the character will be able to see and hear. For example, at the leaving feast in *Philosopher's Stone*, Draco would not be able to hear any of the conversation that might be going on at the Gryffindor table, but he would still hear Dumbledore's speech as it was reported in the book.

❖ In the above example, although Draco would still be able to hear Dumbledore's speech, does that mean that you have to just copy those sections word for word from the book? What other approaches could you use to convey the information?

❖ Think about what the character will know about and what they won't. For example, when Harry, Ron and Hermione enter the Magical Menagerie, Crookshanks won't know their names or who they are. How would Crookshanks refer to the trio?

Scenario information notes

Harry Potter and the Philosopher's Stone   Chapter 17, The Man with Two Faces

Scenario: The end of the chapter, when Harry enters the Great Hall for the end-of-term assembly, Dumbledore awards the last-minute points and Gryffindor wins the House Cup.

Perspective: Re-write this scene from the perspective of Draco Malfoy.

Harry Potter and the Chamber of Secrets   Chapter 2, Dobby's Warning

Scenario: The scene in Harry's bedroom when Dobby arrives to try to persuade Harry not to return to Hogwarts, culminating in the 'pudding incident.'

Perspective: Re-write this scene from the perspective of Dobby.

Harry Potter and the Prisoner of Azkaban   Chapter 4, The Leaky Cauldron

Scenario: Harry, Ron and Hermione enter the Magical Menagerie, a pet shop in Diagon Alley as Ron wants to buy some Rat Tonic for Scabbers. Hermione buys Crookshanks.

Perspective: Re-write this scene from the perspective of Crookshanks.

Harry Potter and the Goblet of Fire   Chapter 23, The Yule Ball

Scenario: Hermione surprises everyone as she arrives at the Yule Ball with her date, Viktor Krum. Ron accuses her of 'consorting with the enemy' and they end the evening by having a blazing argument.

Perspective: Re-write this scene from the perspective of Hermione.

Harry Potter and the Order of the Phoenix   Chapter 1, Dudley Demented

Scenario: Harry joins Dudley as they walk home from the park, and after exchanging some banter the pair are set upon by a pair of Dementors. Harry fights them off, and with Mrs Figg's help, gets Dudley home.

Perspective: Re-write this scene from the perspective of Dudley.

Harry Potter and the Half-Blood Prince   Chapter 13, The Secret Riddle

Scenario: In the pensieve, we see Dumbledore's visit to the Muggle orphanage where Voldemort spent his childhood. Dumbledore meets Tom Riddle, tells him he is a wizard and invites him to Hogwarts.

Perspective: Re-write this scene from the perspective of Tom Riddle.

Harry Potter and the Deathly Hallows   Chapter 19, The Silver Doe

Scenario: Harry dives into the frozen pool to retrieve the sword of Gryffindor but is nearly choked by the locket horcrux. He is saved by Ron who has returned after being guided by the Deluminator. Harry opens the horcrux and Ron destroys it.

Perspective: Re-write this scene from the perspective of Ron.

Ordinary Wizarding Levels

(practice questions)

All students at Hogwarts take Ordinary Wizarding Levels (OWLs) in their fifth year, followed by Nastily Exhausting Wizarding Tests (NEWTs) in their seventh year.

This activity includes a number of questions that might appear on these tests. To answer them, however, students should rely on creativity and imagination rather than hours of Hermione-enforced revision.

Focus area   Creative thinking

Organisation   Students work in small groups

Resources   Copies of **OWL practice questions**
                          Imagination!

What to do

You may choose to present individual practice questions for a quick creative thinking exercise, or all three of them together for a longer session.

Teaching notes on answering the questions

For the first two questions, which are not to be taken too seriously, students should simply be encouraged to give free rein to their imagination and to exercise their sense of humour. The third question requires a more evidence-based response.

❖ **Question 1:** The sky is the limit here. Students should be encouraged to come up with as many divergent responses as possible. Answers could vary from 'an essential ingredient in toothpaste for vampires,' to 'a powerful oven cleaner.'

❖ **Question 2:** Again, imagination and creativity are the key ingredients here. Possible responses could include: Is a great keeper in Quidditch, but only uses his mouth to catch the Quaffle; Walks a circle around his bed three times before going to sleep at night; Doesn't own a towel, he dries off with a vigorous shake after a shower.

❖ **Question 3:** While imagination and creativity are still essential elements, here students must be able to justify their choices. An obvious exception to choose may be money, since we know wizards cannot simply conjure money out of thin air. The cash-strapped Weasley's are evidence of this. The leprechaun gold that rains down on the spectators at the Quidditch World Cup disappears after a few hours. However, what ideas and evidence will students come up with?

OWL practice questions

QUESTION 1: THE TWELVE USES OF DRAGON'S BLOOD

ALBUS DUMBLEDORE, Currently Headmaster of Hogwarts
Considered by many the greatest wizard of modern times, Dumbledore is particularly famous for his defeat of the dark wizard Grindelwald in 1945, for the discovery of the twelve uses of dragon's blood, and his work on alchemy with his partner, Nicholas Flamel. Professor Dumbledore enjoys chamber music and tenpin bowling.

Chocolate Frog Card
Harry Potter and the Philosopher's Stone, Chapter 6

List the twelve uses of dragon's blood.

QUESTION 2: THE TOP FIVE WAYS TO SPOT A WEREWOLF

"'Give five signs that identify the werewolf.' Excellent question."... "One: He's sitting on my chair. Two: He's wearing my clothes. Three: His name's Remus Lupin...."

Lupin discussing the Defence Against the Dark Arts OWL he has just sat
Harry Potter and the Order of the Phoenix, Chapter 28

What are the top five ways to spot a werewolf?

QUESTION 3: GAMP'S LAW OF ELEMENTAL TRANSFIGURATION

"My mother," said Ron ..."can make good food appear out of thin air."
"Your mother can't produce food out of thin air," said Hermione. "No one can. Food is the first of the five Principal Exceptions to Gamp's Law of Elemental Transfigura --"
"Oh, speak English, can't you?" Ron said.

Ron and Hermione while on the run in Wales
Harry Potter and the Deathly Hallows, Chapter 15

If food is the first of the five Principal Exceptions to Gamp's Law of Elemental Transfiguration, what are the other four exceptions? Justify your answers.

Wingardium Leviosa

(the levitation challenge)

One of the first spells we witness Harry and his friends learning at Hogwarts is *Wingardium Leviosa,* the levitation spell, during their Charms lesson in *Philosopher's Stone.* Later, Harry, Ron and Hermione bond while using this spell to fight off the troll in the girls' bathroom.

This activity sets students their own levitation challenge, but without the benefit of a magic wand!

Focus areas   Creative thinking, problem solving

Organisation   Students work in small groups

Resources   One bag or tray per group, each of which contains the same selection of items. Each must contain one feather, or preferably two (artificial ones are available from craft shops), plus a range of other items such as:
- balloons
- paper clips
- string
- assorted magnets
- stiff card
- straws
- elastic bands
- plastic bags
- sticky tape
- any other interesting bits and pieces you have to hand

What to do

1. Organise the students into groups and give each one their bag or tray.

2. Explain the challenge. Using the equipment given, they must find a way to 'levitate' their feather over the greatest distance possible.

Students may touch the feather only once, to set it on its way. Other items may touch the feather, but in that case, students may not touch the item that is touching the feather.

There is no one particular way to solve this challenge - no specific 'answer'. Encourage your students to experiment and try out different ideas. Although there is an element of competition with this activity, stress that you will be awarding points for creativity, as well as for distance.

3. Give the students sufficient time to work on the challenge in their groups.

4. Each group demonstrates their feather levitating skills to the rest of the students.

Agree on demonstration criteria beforehand. For example, each group may be permitted three attempts to demonstrate their method, or to demonstrate two alternative methods. In either case, the attempt that achieves the greatest distance may be taken as their response to the challenge.

Literary Lifeboat

This well-known activity is given a Harry Potter twist, to enable students to develop their skills in reasoned argument.

Focus areas   Language arts (speaking and listening), argument and reason

Organisation   Students work as a whole group

Resources   A set of **character cards** – make your own, with one card or slip of paper for each character

What to do

1. Explain the premise to the students. They will each be representing a character from the Harry Potter series. They are all on a sinking ship and the lifeboat doesn't have enough room for all of them. One of them must be left behind. But who?

2. Students choose a character card out of a hat, to determine which character they will represent. If you are using the character descriptions instead of names, students first have to identify who the character is.

3. In turn, each student tells who they are and gives a brief summary of their role in the books. They then state their case for why their character should be allowed to remain safely in the lifeboat.

4. Once everyone has presented their case, there is a secret vote for who should remain behind. Students write the name of the character they would most like to leave behind on a slip of paper. The votes are counted.

5. The three characters with the highest number of votes take the hot seats. Once again, each one states their case, but the remaining students may now ask questions or challenge their position as well.

6. Everyone votes again for one of the three hot-seated characters. The character with the most votes is deemed to be ejected from the lifeboat.

Note: Encourage students to think deeply about the role of each character in the books and about their choice of who should be left behind. For example, they shouldn't just vote for Dudley Dursley because he is an unpleasant character and they don't like him. Think about his role in the book – not just from a reader's perspective but from a writer's perspective too. How would the story be different if Dudley wasn't in it?

Variation – March Madness

This activity reverses the Literary Lifeboat. Instead of identifying one character to be left behind, this activity forces the students to determine the 'best' or 'most important' character. Since none of the main characters are included, this requires in-depth knowledge of the series and excellent reasoning skills.

What to do

1. Create the brackets for the tournament. You can use an online generator to do this randomly, use the suggested pairings or just create your own.

2. Have students consider what criteria could be used to determine which character is the 'best' or 'most important'. As in the original version of the activity, the aim is to encourage students to carefully consider a character's role in the story and not just vote for their favourite or most popular character.

3. Allocate each student a character, as above.

4. To prepare for round one, each student should prepare a short speech to address how their character meets the criteria of being the best or most important.

5. Each pair of students presents their speech in front of a judging panel of fellow students, who decide on a winner.

6. Round two continues with the winners of the first round. Eliminated students form the judging panels for subsequent rounds. The tournament continues until a winner is decided.

Character cards

A French beauty with seemingly magnetic attraction for many males	A student who is noted for her dedication to divination and kissing
A nosy journalist who likes to bend the truth	A lazy civil servant with a gambling problem
A dreamy student whose father is a newspaper man	A large, somewhat dim boy, much adored by his parents
An elf who was set free with a sock	A red-haired (though balding) civil servant
A hapless teacher who loses her job in a Ministry shake-up	A centaur who is more prepared to talk with humans than most of his kind
An all-round successful student whose life ends tragically	A crusty member of the school staff, who has a cat as his offside
A beautiful student whose friend betrays a resistance movement at the school	The somewhat unpredictable familiar of a very bright witch
An untrustworthy elf who transforms into an ally	A bathroom-haunting ghost

Character names

FLEUR DELACOEUR	LAVENDER BROWN	RITA SKEETER	LUDO BAGMAN
LUNA LOVEGOOD	DUDLEY DURSLEY	DOBBY	ARTHUR WEASLEY
SYBIL TRELAWNEY	FIRENZE	CEDRIC DIGGORY	ARGUS FILCH
CHO CHANG	CROOKSHANKS	KREACHER	MOANING MYRTLE

March Madness Tournament Brackets

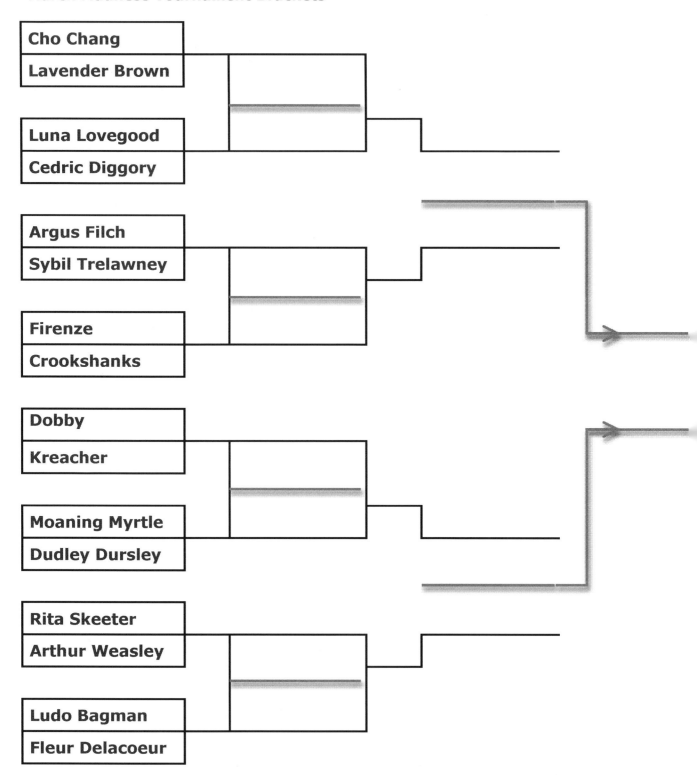

Create your own brackets at: http://challonge.com/tournament/bracket_generator

Hogwarts Staff Meeting
(aka the Great Debate)

In this activity, students will debate some controversial questions related to the Harry Potter series, drawing on their skills of reasoned argument as well as their actual knowledge of the series.

Focus areas   Language arts (speaking and listening), argument and reason

Organisation   Students work as a whole group, divided into two opposing teams

Resources   Your chosen debate topic from the **Great Debate topics,** or your own topic

What to do

1. Divide the students into two opposing teams and advise them of the point of view (affirmative or negative) they will be supporting. Provide the debate topic chosen from the Great Debate topics, or invite students to suggest their own topic, and give the two teams time to prepare their arguments.

2. Arrange the two teams facing each other and toss a coin to decide which team the first speaker will come from. Teams then take turns in presenting their arguments. Every student should participate and have a chance to speak in support of their team.

3. Give all students the chance to cross the floor. If they have been persuaded by the opposing team's arguments, they may express their opinion by voting with their feet.

4. At this point there may be a clear winner and the debate may end here. If the verdict still lies in the balance, however, open the floor for questions. Any student may ask a question of the opposing team but, if possible, questions and answers should proceed in an orderly fashion with the teams taking turns to ask one question.

5. Provide another opportunity to vote and cross the floor. Students are free to change their minds if they wish.

6. Conclude with a discussion of the issues raised and students' reasons for supporting the side they chose.

Great Debate topics
Choose one of these topics or ask students to suggest their own.

Should Slytherin be disbanded?

History shows us that Slytherin has produced more Dark wizards and witches than any other Hogwarts House. This record raises the question, should Slytherin House be disbanded? It is not proposed that Slytherin students be expelled from the school, but that the four Houses become three and that the students from Slytherin be divided amongst the remaining houses equally.

For: Yes, Slytherin House should be disbanded.

Against: No, Slytherin House should remain a part of Hogwarts.

Hermione's S.P.E.W. campaign was misguided

In *Harry Potter and the Goblet of Fire*, Hermione starts a campaign fighting for elf rights. She calls it S.P.E.W. – the Society for the Promotion of Elfish Welfare. She finds it very difficult to drum up support for her campaign and eventually takes to knitting hats and other garments and leaving them around Gryffindor Tower, in the hope that an unsuspecting house-elf will pick them up and be freed. Hermione believes ardently that the slavery-like conditions of the house-elves is wrong, but Ron insists that the elves like to live in this way.

For: Yes, Hermione's campaign was misguided. She should leave the house-elves alone.

Against: No, Hermione's campaign was not misguided. House-elves deserve better conditions, whether they want them or not.

Snape was basically an evil man who did some good things

Even after his death and the end of the series, opinions are still divided over that enigmatic Professor of Potions, Severus Snape. We know that ultimately, like Harry, Snape was Dumbledore's man through and through. However, does that excuse the fact that he made Harry's life a misery, not to mention Neville's, and for displaying incredible bias towards Slytherin?

For: Snape was basically a bad character who did some good things.

Against: No, Snape was basically a good character who did some bad things.

Dynamic Discussion

There is enough material in the Harry Potter series for several years' worth of discussions. Many of the themes in the books lend themselves to thoughtful discussion, leading into the exploration of philosophical issues. Dumbledore's speeches invariably provide plenty of food for thought, as he imparts his considerable wisdom to Harry in each book, but there are also some more light-hearted questions to consider. Discussing literature in this way greatly enhances students' critical reading and thinking skills.

Many of the topics in this activity would also lend themselves to written exploration and could be tackled as essay questions instead.

Focus areas   Language arts (speaking and listening, writing), critical thinking

Organisation   Students work in large or small groups

Resources   Copies of the **Discussion questions**
Paper, reusable sticky notes etc
Quaffle (eg. Basketball or similar)
Reflective journals (optional)

What to do

Various approaches to this in-depth discussion activity are possible, as the suggestions below indicate. The following principles and processes are suggested whatever the particular approach you choose:

❖ The discussion questions provide a starting point for discussion, but do encourage students to suggest their own questions for the group to discuss as well.

❖ Make it clear that your students are not expected to know the answer to these questions (most don't really have an 'answer'), but they are expected to think about them. Encourage them, if they are called on to make a comment, to wonder, to speculate, to think aloud rather than say, 'I don't know.' Of course, it is assumed that you will have already developed an accepting climate in the classroom where students feel safe taking risks like this.

❖ Seat students in a circle or horseshoe shape to allow for easy communication within the group.

❖ Encourage students to do most of the talking. Try to resist the temptation to tell the students what you think, or to ask leading questions. Don't be afraid of silence.

Some suggested approaches to discussion

THINK, PAIR, SHARE

1. Read the chosen question from the **Discussion questions** to the students (displaying it on an interactive whiteboard or handing out copies for students to refer to if you choose).

2. Give them about two minutes of individual thinking time. No one talks; each student just considers the question silently. If you like, they can jot down ideas during this time on sticky notes, individual white boards or in reflective journals.

3. Students discuss the question with their discussion partner for a few minutes. (Arrange the pairings in advance).

4. Call the students back to attention. Having previously written all the students' names on wooden craft sticks (or something similar) and stored them in a cup, you now pick out a student's name at random and ask them to start off the discussion. Put their name back in the cup after you read it. Continue calling on individual students using the name-sticks as the discussion develops.

   The goal of this strategy is to encourage maximum participation, rather than having just a few students dominate the discussion. Because all students have had a chance to both think about the question individually and discuss the question with their partner, it lessens the trepidation they may ordinarily feel if they are called on unexpectedly.

TOSS THE QUAFFLE

1. Read the discussion question and allow a minute or two of thinking time.

2. Toss the quaffle (basketball or something similar) to one of the students.

3. This student gives an initial response to the question, before tossing the quaffle to another student to continue the discussion.

4. Continue in this way, for as long as the students have worthwhile comments to add to the discussion.

DISCUSSION DOODLE

This strategy is good for smaller groups of four to five students; if you have a larger group, you can split them up.

1. With the students around a table, with a large sheet of paper between them, read out the question.

2. As they discuss the question, students doodle. Encourage them to sketch images and symbols, as well as to write words or phrases. As the discussion progresses, the group will develop a giant doodle demonstrating their ideas, trains of though and thinking processes.

3. If you have split up a larger group for this activity, each small group can share their doodles with the larger group.

REFLECTIVE JOURNAL

Whichever approach to group discussion you take, you may like to encourage students to keep a reflective journal in which to note down their thoughts and ideas after each discussion. Allow ten minutes or so at the end of the session for students to write in their journal while the ideas are still fresh in their mind. This might also be an opportunity for students to think of questions of their own they would like to pursue.

Discussion questions

1

"The truth is a beautiful and terrible thing, and should therefore be treated with great caution."

Professor Dumbledore
Harry Potter and the Philosopher's Stone, Chapter 17

Discuss what Dumbledore means by this.

2

"It is our choices Harry, that show what we truly are, far more than our abilities."

Professor Dumbledore
Harry Potter and the Chamber of Secrets, Chapter 18

Do you agree with Dumbledore's statement?

3

The prophecy in *Harry Potter and the Order of the Phoenix* could have applied to either Harry or Neville.

What if Voldemort had chosen Neville instead?
Could Neville have become the man Harry became?
Could he have defeated Voldemort?

4

Are any characters in the series completely evil or completely good?

5

Consider these two opposing quotes – one from the first book and one from the final book.

"There is no good or evil, there is only power, and those too weak to seek it."

Professor Quirrel
Harry Potter and the Philosopher's Stone, Chapter 17

"...perhaps those who are best suited to power are those who have never sought it."

Professor Dumbledore
Harry Potter and the Deathly Hallows, Chapter 35

Discuss

6

... and in March several of the mandrakes threw a loud and raucous party in Greenhouse Three.

Harry Potter and the Chamber of Secrets, Chapter 14

What would a mandrake do during a party?

7

Who is the better friend to Harry – Ron or Hermione? Why?

What makes a good friend?

8

"Of course it is happening inside your head, Harry, but why on earth should that mean it is not real?"

Professor Dumbledore
Harry Potter and the Deathly Hallows, Chapter 35

Discuss

9

In the final book, Harry uses two Unforgivable Curses.

In some circumstances, are normally unforgivable actions forgivable?

Is it forgivable to do unforgivable things for the greater good?

10

Consider these lines from the Sorting Hat's song in Chapter 12 of *Harry Potter and the Goblet of Fire*, explaining how the four founders of Hogwarts houses chose the members for their own house:

> *...for each*
> *Did value different virtues*
> *In the ones they had to teach.*
> *By Gryffindor, the bravest were*
> *Prized far beyond the rest;*
> *For Ravenclaw, the cleverest*
> *Would always be the best;*
> *For Hufflepuff, hard workers were*
> *Most worthy of ambition;*
> *And power-hungry Slytherin*
> *Loved those of great ambition.*

Is ambition a virtue?

Riddikulus Riddles

Riddles are an ancient form of poetry, with one of the earliest known examples being that of the Sphinx to Oedipus from Greek mythology. J.K Rowling gave us her version when Harry came face to face with the Sphinx in the maze in *Goblet of Fire*. In this activity, students will be challenged to solve some Harry Potter related riddles, before attempting to create one of their own.

Focus areas	Language arts (reading, writing), critical and creative thinking
Organisation	Students work in pairs or small groups
Resources	Copies of **Riddles** Copies of **Riddle solutions** Copies of **How to write a riddle guidelines**

What to do

1. You could use these riddles in several different ways. For example you could:

   o Present all the riddles in one longer session, challenging students to solve them, studying the solutions, then creating a riddle of their own

   o Present the riddles individually – perhaps as a riddle of the day or a riddle of the week, with a small prize for the first student to solve it

   o Present the riddles individually in shorter sessions, when students work together to try to solve the riddle and then study its solution, leading up to a culminating riddle-writing activity session.

2. However the riddles are introduced, once the answer has been revealed, share the full solution with students so they can examine the language features and structure more fully.

3. Give students a copy of the **How to write a riddle guidelines** and have them work together to create a riddle of their own.

4. Students challenge each other with their own riddles.

Riddles

Riddle No. 1	Many hands make light work but my work is never-ending. Time and again I tell you what you need to know But I don't tell you what I should. Who or what am I?
Riddle No. 2	My story is quite gory but I can't take all the credit If you ask, I shall not bask, so you might as well forget it I'm partial to a drink and my appetite is hearty but you will never find me in the kitchen at a party Who or what am I?
Riddle No. 3	Face the facts I'm the cause of failure, On the fringes of a famous family But not all of me. I'm not wrong, But I might not be right either!

Riddle No. 4	I helped you go from here to there, Now I won't take you anywhere. There was no trust without the tea, Innocent victims fell with me. I was so young, it's such a shame, But Voldemort must take the blame.
Riddle No. 5	My first sounds like Professor Sprout But the start we can do without. Replace the beginning instead With what's in red but not in bed. My second speaks of creatures three Who played their part, but not with me. After that comes the sound you make When you have no words to take. Finally, I make the sound Of that which burrows underground. Put them together and you will see That you have discovered me!
Riddle No. 6	With features like mine I could work in a bar, But my half-blood status means I'll go far. A Weasley? Not me. But I could be. Not Harry's left foot, but a petty criminal's lower leg.

Riddle solutions

Riddle No. 1

ANSWER: The Weasley Clock (Mrs Weasley's unique clock which tells her where each member of the family is at any given time)

MANY HANDS MAKE LIGHT WORK BUT MY WORK IS NEVER-ENDING.
This first line is a play on the popular **idiom** *many hands make light work*. The 'many hands' is a clue because the Weasley Clock has a lot more hands than a regular clock. A clock's work never ends.
TIME AND AGAIN I TELL YOU WHAT YOU NEED TO KNOW
BUT I DON'T TELL YOU WHAT I SHOULD.
The key clue here is 'time' which hints at the clock, but this clock doesn't tell the time, like most clocks do, so it doesn't tell you what it should, but the information it gives instead is far more useful.

Riddle No. 2

ANSWER: Sanguini (the vampire Harry meets at Slughorn's Christmas party in *Half-Blood Prince*)

MY STORY IS QUITE GORY
The story in question being 'Blood Brothers: My Life Amongst the Vampires'
BUT I CAN'T TAKE ALL THE CREDIT
The book was actually written by Eldred Worple, who also offered to write Harry's story for him
IF YOU ASK, I SHALL NOT BASK
SO YOU MIGHT AS WELL FORGET IT
Bask is of course a **synonym** for sunbathe, and vampires are known to shun the sun
I'M PARTIAL TO A DRINK AND MY APPETITE IS HEARTY
'Hearty' is a bit of a **double entendre** here. First of all vampires drink blood, and blood is pumped around the body by the heart.
BUT YOU WILL NEVER FIND ME IN THE KITCHEN AT A PARTY.
Of course not, that's where they keep the garlic! Also a nod to the fact that we meet Sanguini at a party, which takes place in Slughorn's room.

ANSWER: The half of Ron Weasley's eyebrow (that caused him to fail his Apparition test)

FACE THE FACTS
The key word here is 'face' - a big clue!

I'M THE CAUSE OF FAILURE
The half-eyebrow left behind was the reason Ron failed his Apparition test.

ON THE FRINGES OF A FAMOUS FAMILY.
'Fringe' is a hint that hair is involved. In fact, a dictionary **definition** of eyebrow is 'a fringe of hair above the eye'. Famous family obviously refers to the Weasleys.

BUT NOT ALL OF ME.
We're only talking about half of the eyebrow, not all of it!

I'M NOT WRONG,
BUT I MIGHT NOT BE RIGHT EITHER.
This clue relies on a **pun**. If something is not wrong, and not right, then it must be left! Actually, we aren't told whether it was Ron's right or left eyebrow that caused the problem, so these two lines hint at that.

ANSWER: The Brockdale Bridge (referred to by the Muggle Prime Minister in Chapter 1 of *Half Blood Prince*)

I HELPED YOU GO FROM HERE TO THERE,
Well, that's what a bridge does! This and the following line is a **literal** clue to the solution.

NOW I WON'T TAKE YOU ANYWHERE.
The bridge was broken, snapped in two, so it won't take you anywhere anymore.

THERE WAS NO TRUST WITHOUT THE TEA,
This is a **cryptic** clue. Take the T from trust and you're left with rust. The Muggle PM had to answer questions about rusted rigging, but there was no rust on the bridge.

INNOCENT VICTIMS FELL WITH ME.
Over a dozen cars fell to the river below when the bridge snapped in two.

I WAS SO YOUNG, IT'S SUCH A SHAME,
The bridge was less than 10 years old.

BUT VOLDEMORT MUST TAKE THE BLAME.
Voldemort was actually responsible for the bridge's collapse.

Riddle No. 5

ANSWER: Reg Cattermole (the Ministry of Magic worker impersonated by Ron in the trio's daring infiltration of the Ministry in *Deathly Hallows*)

MY FIRST SOUNDS LIKE PROFESSOR SPROUT
BUT THE START WE CAN DO WITHOUT.
REPLACE THE BEGINNING INSTEAD
WITH WHAT'S IN RED BUT NOT IN BED.

This is a classic riddle structure where the clues refer to the sound of the word rather than the whole. These first four lines refer to Reg. Sprout is a type of vegetable, a word which is commonly shortened to veg. Replace the beginning letter V with an R (the only letter in red but not in bed), and you have Reg.

MY SECOND SPEAKS OF CREATURES THREE
WHO PLAYED THEIR PART, BUT NOT WITH ME.

Cats! There are three cats in the series - Mrs. Norris, Crookshanks and Mr. Tibbles. All have their part to play but none are involved with Reg.

AFTER THAT COMES THE SOUND YOU MAKE
WHEN YOU HAVE NO WORDS TO TAKE.

This part is heavily influenced by the sphinx's riddle in the maze. 'Er' is what you say when you don't know what to say.

FINALLY, I MAKE THE SOUND
OF THAT WHICH BURROWS UNDERGROUND.

Not the magical Niffler but the more mundane mole.

PUT THEM TOGETHER AND YOU WILL SEE
THAT YOU HAVE DISCOVERED ME!

Reg + cat + er + mole = Reg Cattermole!

Riddle No. 6

ANSWER: Crookshanks

WITH FEATURES LIKE MINE I COULD WORK IN A BAR,

Crookshanks is described as having a bottlebrush tail which would undoubtedly come in handy for cleaning bottles at the Hogs Head - much better than Aberforth's dirty rag.

BUT MY HALF-BLOOD STATUS MEANS I'LL GO FAR.

Crookshanks is half Kneazle, and they have an excellent sense of direction.

A WEASLEY?
NOT ME.
BUT I COULD BE.

With Crookshanks' ginger fur (hair) he'd fit right in with the Weasley family.

NOT HARRY'S LEFT FOOT, BUT A PETTY CRIMINAL'S LOWER LEG.

The **cryptic**, but giveaway clue! Petty criminal = crook + lower leg = shank (more commonly applied to animals, as in lamb shanks).

How to Write a Riddle

Like most forms of poetry, there are no hard and fast rules for writing a riddle, so be as creative as you like. Some rhyme, some don't. Some are short, some are longer. Some follow a pattern, like the Sphinx's riddle from Goblet of Fire, or Riddle No. 5, of describing the sound of the word or individual syllables rather than the thing itself. Others personify the subject of the riddle within its whole form. Whatever form it takes, the mark of a good riddle is that it seems obvious once you know the answer.

To get started with creating your own riddle, follow these steps.

1. First choose the subject of your riddle. This could be a character, an object, a place or even an event from the Harry Potter series.

2. Next, brainstorm a list of words or phrases that come to mind when you think about your subject. Think of descriptive words that could refer to physical attributes, personality traits, actions or significance in the story.

3. Use a dictionary and thesaurus to look up alternative words and synonyms for some of your descriptions.

4. Be alert for homonyms and homophones which you might use in your descriptions. These can be helpful when it comes to creating puns. For example, if the subject of your riddle was Black (as in Sirius), you might play on the homophones mourning/morning, as follows:

   You'll see me in morning and also at night
   You'll see me in shadows away from the light

5. Look for ways to incorporate other figurative language, such as similes and metaphor in your descriptions.

6. Put some of your descriptions together into a verse and see how they sound. Don't worry too much about rhyme at this stage. Just look for how the riddle flows.

7. Play around with it until you're happy with the result.

8. Try it out on someone!

Wizard Wordplay

The quick activities in this section are designed to give students opportunities to play around with language, while developing their critical thinking skills. Use them whenever you have five or ten minutes to fill, or explore them in more depth if you have more time.

Focus areas   Language arts (writing), critical thinking

Organisation   Students could work individually, in pairs or small groups

Resources   Copies of **Read all about it suggestions**

Read all about it!

The wizarding world seems to have two main sources of news – the *Daily Prophet* and the *Quibbler*. Both have a very different style and approach to reporting the news. In this activity, students are challenged to write a headline for the same incident for each newspaper.

1. Refer students to a newsworthy event. This could be:
   o A specific chapter from one of the books
   o One of the suggested events
   o An event of your own choosing

2. Ask students to write two headlines for the event – one that might appear in the Daily Prophet, and one in keeping with the style of the Quibbler.

Variation: Instead of headlines, ask the students to write a Tweet in the style of a particular character.

Read all about it suggestions

The fight in Flourish & Blotts between Mr Weasley and Mr Malfoy	The sacking of Sybil Trelawney	The Dementor attack on Harry and Dudley in Little Whinging
The disappearance of Florean Fortescue	Hagrid's experiment breeding blast-ended skrewts	The escape of the Gringott's dragon
Any of the Hogwarts quidditch matches	The arrest of Stan Shunpike	The second task of the Triwizard Tournament
Gilderoy Lockhart's admission to St. Mungo's with severe amnesia	The passing of Educational Decree No. 27 (any student found in possession of the Quibbler will be expelled)	The appointment of Rufus Scrimgeour as Minister for Magic

Harry Potter in 99 words

A deceptively simple activity, yet one which forces students to write concisely and think very carefully about word choice.

1. Allocate students one of the seven books in the series and challenge them to write a synopsis of the story in exactly 99 words – no more, no less.

2. Make this more challenging by asking them to summarise the entire series in just 99 words.

The Last Word

Before the publication of the final book, J.K. Rowling famously gave an interview where she revealed that the last word in the last book was 'scar.' Sometime prior to publication, she changed her mind! However, in a variation of the popular creative writing exercise where students are given a first line as a prompt, this activity gives students the last word, and challenges them to write a passage to fit predetermined parameters. Write:

o A 50 word story, with the last word being 'scar.'

o A 100 word story, with the first word 'Waving' and the last word 'relieved.'

o A 150 word story, where the first word is 'Black', the 75th word is 'Muggle' and the last word is 'always.'

The possibilities are endless! Come up with some of your own.

Harry Potter and the Learning Ladders

These learning ladders are designed to provide students with a range of thought-provoking activities to enhance their understanding and enjoyment of each book in the series. Loosely based on the ideas of both Bloom's Taxonomy and Gardner's Multiple Intelligences, they are also influenced by the three-level ladder developed by Wilson and Murdoch (2008).

Focus areas   Multiple

Organisation   Students work individually, or in pairs, or possibly as a whole group

Resources   Copies of the **Learning Ladder** designed for the Harry Potter book you are focusing on
Other resources as required by the specific activity

What to do

There are really many different ways in which you can use these learning ladders. For example, you might use them:

o   as an individual contract if you only have one Harry Potter reader in your class who needs some extension

o   with groups of students who can work on the activities individually or in pairs, either in class time or as homework assignments

o   as a whole group exercise, focusing on individual activities you have picked out to do in a more in-depth way.

As a guide, it is suggested that students complete at least three activities from each Ladder, one from each row. However, as this approach is flexible as well, students may well choose to do more than three.

Learning Ladder: Harry Potter and the Philosopher's Stone

Starting at the bottom, choose at least one activity from each row. Your three responses then show (1) what you know or understand; (2) how you can analyse or organize information; and (3) how you can be creative.

LEARNING FOCUS	WORD	MATHEMATICAL	VISUAL	MUSICAL	TACTILE
3 CREATE	Was Dumbledore being honest when he told Harry what he saw in the Mirror of Erised? What do you think he saw? What would you see?	Create a floor plan of one room in Hogwarts, eg. The Great Hall, Gryffindor's common room, Harry's dormitory. Include a scale.	Choose a scene from the book to illustrate. Would it be a suitable choice for the front cover? Why or why not?	Record yourself reading an extract from the book. Add suitable sound effects and background music.	Create a board game using the events of the book as a guide.
2 APPLY / ANALYSE	Create a glossary explaining the meanings of all the new words we learn in this book.	Create 10 money problems using wizard currency – eg. How many Knuts in 10 galleons? Include an answer sheet.	Draw a Venn diagram to compare and contrast two characters from the book, eg. Harry and Draco.	List five songs you would find on Harry's iPod and explain your choices. Choose another character and do the same.	Design a Muggle version of Quidditch that can be played on the ground. Explain the rules and include a diagram.
1 KNOW / UNDERSTAND	Write the letters A-Z down the left-hand side of your page. Try to find at least one word related to this book for each letter of the alphabet.	How many students do you think there are at Hogwarts? Use evidence from the book to justify your answer.	List all the information you can learn about the book from the front and back covers (not including the blurb).	List all the information we can learn about Hogwarts from the Sorting Hat song and the school song.	Watch the film. How does it differ from the book? Why do you think it differs in these ways?

Learning Ladder: Harry Potter and the Chamber of Secrets

Starting at the bottom, choose at least one activity from each row. Your three responses then show (1) what you know or understand; (2) how you can analyse or organize information; and (3) how you can be creative.

LEARNING FOCUS	WORD	MATHEMATICAL	VISUAL	MUSICAL	TACTILE
CREATE (3)	Write the first chapter of Gilderoy Lockhart's autobiography, *Magical Me*.	Draw a map of Diagon Alley and Knockturn Alley, showing the location of shops and other buildings we know of.	Create an alternative front cover that gives different information to that available from the cover(s) you have seen.	Create a 'mix tape' containing a collection of music that could be played at the Deathday Party.	Make a model of The Burrow using whatever materials you like.
APPLY / ANALYSE (2)	Imagine Lockhart sent himself a singing Valentine. What would it say?	Make a timeline of events from when Harry was born to the events of this book.	Compare and contrast two of the covers that have been used for this book.	List five songs that you think you would find on Gilderoy Lockhart's iPod. Explain your choices.	Keep a diary of your own for a week.
KNOW / UNDERSTAND (1)	Collect as much information as possible on Gilderoy Lockhart. Present it as a list of facts.	Use information given in Chapter 8, *The Deathday Party*, to work out the year in which the events in this book are taking place.	Collect at least three different images of cover art for this book. What information does each cover give?	Find a piece of music that you think could represent phoenix song.	Have a conversation with Tom Riddle's diary online at: http://goo.gl/fgt379

Learning Ladder: Harry Potter and the Prisoner of Azkaban

Starting at the bottom, choose at least one activity from each row. Your three responses then show (1) what you know or understand; (2) how you can analyse or organize information; and (3) how you can be creative.

LEARNING FOCUS	WORD	MATHEMATICAL	VISUAL	MUSICAL	TACTILE
3 CREATE	What if Buckbeak had been found innocent? Create a new ending using a flowchart or a story map.	Using information from the first three books, create your own version of the Marauders Map.	Create a visual way of showing the timeline of events in the time travel episode.	Create an original piece of music that could be used to signify the presence of Dementors.	Make an original advertisement for the Knight Bus, suitable for TV, radio or print.
2 APPLY / ANALYSE	Sirius was freed by Harry & Hermione on 6 June. Find out what happened on this date in 1944. Are there examples of more coinciding dates in this and the other books in the series?	Make a pie chart showing a typical day at Hogwarts for Harry. Do the same for Hermione. Compare the two charts.	Design a new Wanted poster for Sirius Black that reflects what we learn about him in this book.	Harry misses the Sorting in this book. Write a song that the Sorting Hat might have sung in this year.	Find some willing volunteers and attempt to read their tea leaves.
1 KNOW / UNDERSTAND	List all the clues you can find that hint at Remus Lupin being a werewolf.	Make a series of math problems based on the Knight Bus fares. Include an answer sheet.	Choose one of the characters we meet for the first time in this book and draw this character.	Listen to the soundtrack of the film version of this book. Which piece of music is your favourite? Why?	Research the art of telling the future through reading tea leaves.

Learning Ladder: Harry Potter and the Goblet of Fire

Starting at the bottom, choose at least one activity from each row. Your three responses then show (1) what you know or understand; (2) how you can analyse or organize information; and (3) how you can be creative.

LEARNING FOCUS	WORD	MATHEMATICAL	VISUAL	MUSICAL	TACTILE
CREATE	Imagine you are a student of Beauxbatons or Durmstrang. Write a letter home describing some of your time at Hogwarts.	Construct a table showing what might have been the results from the Quidditch World Cup qualifying rounds. Include the information given in the book.	Create a poster to advertise the Triwizard Tournament.	Write an extra wizard-type verse for either the Irish or the Bulgarian anthem. Do the same for the anthem of your own country.	Design what could be a fourth task for the Triwizard Tournament and find a creative way to present your idea.
APPLY / ANALYSE	Use a mind map or a flow chart to organize the most important elements of the plot of this book.	How much would Harry's 1000 galleon prize money weigh if 1 galleon is worth £5 (or convert to your own currency) and it has the same value as gold, gram for gram? Give answers for 9ct, 18ct and 24ct gold.	Consider the colours associated with each House. Why do you think J.K. Rowling chose those colours in each case?	Choose five songs that the Weird Sisters might have played at the Yule Ball. Justify your choices.	Create a maze and challenge some other students or your teacher to solve it. How long does it take them?
KNOW / UNDERSTAND	List all the information we learn about Beauxbatons and Durmstrang. What other questions do you still have about these schools.	How much would the Weasley twins have won if Bagman gave them odds of : 30 – 1 50 – 1 66 – 1 (Don't forget the funny wand.)	Find several examples of promotional posters for the *Goblet of Fire* film. Describe the elements they have in common.	Find the lyrics for the Irish and Bulgarian national anthems. What do they have in common?	Identify a scene from the film that differs from how you imagined it when reading the book. Describe how you would have filmed it if you were the director.

Learning Ladder: Harry Potter and the Order of the Phoenix

Starting at the bottom, choose at least one activity from each row. Your three responses then show (1) what you know or understand; (2) how you can analyse or organize information; and (3) how you can be creative.

LEARNING FOCUS	WORD	MATHEMATICAL	VISUAL	MUSICAL	TACTILE
CREATE (3)	"Remember my last, Petunia." Write Dumbledore's last letter to Petunia Dursley.	Using your imagination, as well as information from the book, create a graph to show the circulation figures of *The Quibbler* for the year and analyse the trends.	Create a t-shirt design that could be worn by **either** a member of Dumbledore's Army **or** the Order of the Phoenix.	In a similar style to 'Weasley is our King,' write a song or chant for another member of the Gryffindor team and one for a Slytherin team member.	Construct a board game or similar based on the events that happen in the Department of Mysteries.
APPLY / ANALYSE (2)	Choose a moment in the story and write a diary entry for it as Dolores Umbridge.	On a map of the United Kingdom, devise a key and use your best guesses to show all the journeys Harry makes this year.	Design a poster with a suitable message to display at St. Mungo's, eg. 'A clean cauldron keeps potions from becoming poisons.'	Could Sirius Black really have been Stubby Boardman, lead singer of the Hobgoblins? Present arguments for and against.	With a partner, enact the scene between McGonagall and Umbridge after Harry leaves his careers advice interview.
KNOW / UNDERSTAND (1)	Using information given in Chapter 7 and later in the book, compile a brochure that provides a visitor's guide to the Ministry of Magic.	Take an online Harry Potter quiz at: http://goo.gl/myiqms	Examine as many different covers as you can find for this book. Can you identify which scene inspired each one?	Read the Sorting Hat's new song. Rephrase the information given and present it in another format.	Re-create one of Dolores Umbridge's ornamental plates, using a paper plate and other materials of your choice.

Learning Ladder: Harry Potter and the Half-Blood Prince

Starting at the bottom, choose at least one activity from each row. Your three responses then show (1) what you know or understand; (2) how you can analyse or organize information; and (3) how you can be creative.

LEARNING FOCUS	WORD	MATHEMATICAL	VISUAL	MUSICAL	TACTILE
CREATE	Write the back cover blurb for *Blood Brothers: My Life Amongst the Vampires* by Eldred Worple.	Investigate the use of products sold in Weasley's Wizard Wheezes. Design the packaging and an advertisement for it to publish in the Daily Prophet.	Choose one of the lyrics to Celestina Warbeck's 'A Cauldron Full of Hot, Strong Love' (Chapter 16) and set it to music.	Write the rest of the family a version of Mrs Weasley's clock, which tells her when the family are 'in mortal peril.'	Create for your own
APPLY / ANALYSE	"Dumbledore says people find it far easier to forgive others for being wrong than being right." (Chapter 5) Discuss this statement.	Draw a floor plan of Weasley's Wizard Wheezes, using a scale, a key and as much information from the book as possible.	Design a new cover for Harry's battered copy of Advanced Potion Making.	Choose a song that might have been played at Dumbledore's funeral. Explain your choice.	Make a scrapbook containing images, artifacts and/or words to recount the main events of the book.
KNOW / UNDERSTAND	Re-tell the main events of the book using 150 words or less.	Make a timeline of the memories Dumbledore shows Harry in the pensieve.	Create a visual flow chart of the various student pairings and relationships this year.	Harry misses the Sorting Hat's song again but asks what it said. Write a verse or two that the Hat might have sung at the feast.	Identify and describe the main differences between the book and the film. What are the impacts of these changes?

Learning Ladder: Harry Potter and the Deathly Hallows

Starting at the bottom, choose at least one activity from each row. Your three responses then show (1) what you know or understand; (2) how you can analyse or organize information; and (3) how you can be creative.

LEARNING FOCUS	WORD	MATHEMATICAL	VISUAL	MUSICAL	TACTILE
CREATE	Write an extra chapter that tells the story of the attempted theft of Gryffindor's sword by Neville, Ginny and Luna.	Scrimgeour thought Dumbledore had left a coded message for Hermione. Devise a code and use it to write such a message.	Design a set of commemorative coins, including a galleon, sickle and knut, celebrating the events of the book. Include both sides of each coin.	Write and record a program for *Potterwatch*, including theme music or jingle.	Imagine a future time when sales of *Deathly Hallows* are slipping. Design and make a free gift to be given away with the book to boost sales.
APPLY / ANALYSE	What parallels can be drawn between the events of the *Deathly Hallows* and the Second World War?	Rate each chapter on criteria of your choice, eg. Suspense and excitement. Plot the results on a graph.	Compare the original Bloomsbury and Scholastic covers of the book. Why do you think they chose such different scenes? Which do you prefer? Why?	Choose five characters and give them *Potterwatch* nicknames. Explain your choices.	Design and make a chocolate frog card for at least two of the following characters: Dobby; Severus Snape; Gellert Grindelwald.
KNOW / UNDERSTAND	Starting with Hedwig, we lose a lot of characters in this book. Write an obituary column that includes all the characters who don't survive.	Using a ruler and a compass, draw the *Deathly Hallows* symbol in a range of sizes. Develop a formula to calculate the area of each space within the symbol.	Make an illustrated children's book telling the *Tale of the Three Brothers*.	Modify an existing song to retell the events of one or more chapters in the book.	Do you agree with the film-makers' choice of where to split the book to make the two *Deathly Hallows* films? Why or why not? Where would you have chosen to split it? Explain?

Recommended Websites

The website addresses given in this book are correct at the time of publication. However, website addresses can change, and some websites may adopt advertising that is inappropriate for the classroom. It is therefore advisable to check each website you plan to use in the classroom before actually using it with your students. The author takes no responsibility for the content of any website included in this book.

The Harry Potter Alliance Thehpalliance.org	This army of fans, activists, nerdfighters, teenagers, wizards and Muggles is dedicated to fighting for social justice with the greatest weapon we have – love.
The Harry Potter Lexicon www.hp-lexicon.info	Information and minute details from the series arranged in an encyclopaedic fashion. A great resource.
The Harry Potter Wiki Harrypotter.wikia.com	All kinds of minutiae concerning everything to do with Harry Potter. A great search function.
The Leaky Cauldron The-leaky-cauldron.org	Lots of news and features, including its own version of *The Quibbler*, regular competitions and the largest Harry Potter social network on the internet.
Mugglenet www.mugglenet.com	Features news, views, forums, discussions and podcasts with sections for fanfiction and fanart too.
J.K. Rowling Official Site www.jkrowling.com	News of the author and her various projects.
Pottermore www.pottermore.com	J.K. Rowling's newest venture. An online interactive experience built from the reading of the Harry Potter series.
Internet Anagram Server www.wordsmith.org/anagram	A great resource to use for the anagram activities
Anagram Genius www.anagramgenius.com	A great resource to use for the anagram activities

References and further resources

Anelli, M. (2008) *Harry, A History: The true story of a boy wizard, his fans, and life inside the Harry Potter phenomenon.* New York: Pocket Books.

Baggett, D. & Klein, S.E. (Eds.) (2004) *Harry Potter and Philosophy: If Aristotle ran Hogwarts.* Chicago: Open Court.

Dweck, C. (2012) *Mindset: How you can fulfill your potential.* London: Constable and Robinson.

Gladwell, M. (2008) *Outliers: The story of success.* London: Penguin.

Halstead, J.W. (2009) *Some of my best friends are books: Guiding gifted readers from preschool to high school,* 3rd Edition. Scottsdale, AZ: Great Potential Press.

Gibbs, N.(2007) J.K.Rowling. *TIME* Magazine, 19 December 2007, accessed online at: http://www.time.com/time/specials/2007/personoftheyear/0,28757,1690753,00.html #ixzz1KdDW1Wf3

Gross, M.U.M., Macleod, B., Drummond, D. & Merrick, C. (2003) *Gifted students in primary schools: Differentiating the curriculum.* Sydney: Gifted Education Research, Resource and Information Centre (GERRIC).

Mathew, K.L. & Adams, D.C. (2009) I love your book, but I love my version more: Fanfiction in the English language arts classroom. *The ALAN Review, 36*:3, 35-41.

Powell, W. & Kusuma-Powell, O. (2011) *How to teach now: Five keys to personalised learning in the global classroom.* ASCD: Alexandria, VA.

Rowling, J.K. (1997) *Harry Potter and the Philosopher's Stone.* London: Bloomsbury.

Rowling, J.K. (1998) *Harry Potter and the Chamber of Secrets.* London: Bloomsbury.

Rowling, J.K. (1999) *Harry Potter and the Prisoner of Azkaban.* London: Bloomsbury.

Rowling, J.K. (2000) *Harry Potter and the Goblet of Fire.* London: Bloomsbury.

Rowling, J.K. (2001) *Fantastic Beasts and Where to Find Them.* London: Bloomsbury.

Rowling, J.K. (2003). *Harry Potter and the Order of the Phoenix.* London: Bloomsbury

Rowling, J.K. (2005) *Harry Potter and the Half-Blood Prince.* London: Bloomsbury.

Rowling, J.K. (2007) *Harry Potter and the Deathly Hallows.* London. Bloomsbury.

Vogler, Christopher (1992) *The Writer's Journey: Mythic Structure for Storytellers and Screenwriters.* Studio City, CA.: Michael Wiese Productions.

Wilson, J. & Murdoch, K. (2008) *Learning for themselves.* Victoria, Australia: Curriculum Corporation.

About the author

Selena Gallagher is a teacher who has worked with gifted students in Australia, the UK, China and Thailand. After completing a PhD in gifted education, she is working on developing gifted education programs in international schools. Selena discovered Harry Potter in 2001 and became instantly hooked. She has been developing and delivering Harry related activities to gifted learners for the past eight years. She is still secretly hoping that her Hogwarts letter has been lost in the post.

Printed in Great Britain
by Amazon